WHAT IS LIBERAL SOCIALISM?

Matt McManus

WHAT IS LIBERAL SOCIALISM?

Matt McManus

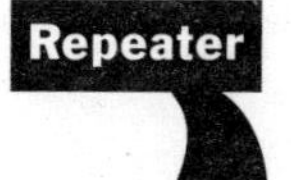

Published by Repeater Books

An imprint of Watkins Media Ltd

Unit 11 Shepperton House

89-93 Shepperton Road

London

N1 3DF

United Kingdom

www.repeaterbooks.com

A Repeater Books paperback original 2026

1

Distributed in the United States by Random House, Inc., New York.

Copyright Matt McManus © 2026

Matt McManus asserts the moral right to be identified as the author of this work.

ISBN: 9781917516419

Ebook ISBN: 9781917516426

The manufacturer's authorised representative in the EU for product safety is: eucomply OÜ - Pärnu mnt 139b-14, 11317 Tallinn, Estonia, hello@eucompliancepartner.com, www.eucompliancepartner.com

Printed and bound by CPI Group (UK) Ltd, Croydon, CR0 4YY

*Dedicated to Brendan and James
in Friendship and Solidarity*

CONTENTS

ACKNOWLEDGEMENTS

The essays in this collection were reprinted with the permission of *Jacobin, Aeon Magazine, Damage Magazine, Liberal Currents* and others. Many of the editors worked hard to improve them, including: Nick French, Paul Crider, Adam Gurri, Benjamin Feng, Sam Dresser and others. Any remaining mistakes are of course my own. Gratitude should also be extended to Routledge Press, the publisher of *The Political Theory of Liberal Socialism*. Thank you very much to my wife, Marion Trejo, and my family: John, Jean, Emily, Meagan, Adam, Kayla, Chris and Matt. Finally, much love to all my friends and colleagues, including Brendan and James, to whom this collection is dedicated.

PREFACE

To the reader who is not sufficiently ideologically aligned, the use of the term *liberal socialism* may bring many things to mind — except the idea that this is a political-theoretical worldview characterized by coherence and consistency. A worldview that makes any form of intellectual engagement (not only from a political-activist perspective but also from a theoretical/philosophical perspective) seem like a worthwhile endeavour.

Rather, the intuitive impression may initially arise that we are dealing with an insurmountable form of contradiction — a circumstance that provides not least an explanation as to why it does seem plausible that the use of the term *liberal socialism* is capable of provoking a great deal of indignation.[1]

However, to dismiss the political theory of liberal socialism as a mere oxymoron reveals more about the increasingly tribalized state of contemporary discourse than it does about the nuances of liberal socialist theory itself. This knee-jerk rejection stems, in no small part, from the way tribalistic tendencies function within the political sphere — regardless of one's chosen political camp. These tendencies rely on a strict adherence to an ideologically closed worldview, one that is inherently static and decoupled from

---

1   Cf. Matt McManus, *The Political Theory of Liberal Socialism*, Routledge 2025, 1.

any form of critical reflexivity. In short — and perhaps somewhat provocatively, whether one fervently believes in the ultimate triumph of liberalism, envisioning it as the "end of history," or conversely, anticipates the inevitable demise of the liberal project (and the victory of the socialist project) is ultimately a question — according to this particular reading — that is often approached with a rigid, *either/or* mentality, negating any possibility of synthesis or compromise

Another objection one might be inclined to raise against the terminological (and normative) implications of liberal socialism is that it suggests a certain indecisiveness at the theoretical level. It's like being willing to commit to a monogamous relationship — *but only if affairs are allowed!* Or being prepared to eat vegetarian — *as long as you can eat meat at least once or twice on the weekend!* It's like living a teetotal life, opposing the consumption of alcohol — *yet indulging in two bottles of wine every evening!* Or — more relevantly — it's like finding liberal-democratic principles and the protection of pluralistic interests wonderful, *but having a few interests where a dictatorial approach seems sensible, (because they seem so important to one's worldview) to be sure they are implemented!*

Matthew McManus, through his numerous essayistic interventions in recent years, has clearly emphasized that such accusations misunderstand the political theory of liberal socialism and, more importantly, the beneficial, emancipatory implications it holds for current discussions in both political theory and progressive activism.

In addition to numerous essayistic interventions — many of which can be found in collected form in this book — McManus' recent book project, *The Political Theory of Liberal Socialism*, published by Routledge in 2025, deserves a special mention. Here he develops a "retrieval" — as he puts it with reference to C.B. Macpherson[2] — of the liberal socialist project. McManus' work in this area cannot be overestimated — which is why I was more than grateful when I was asked by the journal *Contemporary Political Theory* to write a review of his brilliant book. Since I fully share McManus' ambitions for the liberal socialist project, I am even more pleased to be able to contribute to this collection of essays.

Liberalism faces worldwide attacks from diverse political camps — a point that cannot be emphasized enough. The political theory of liberal socialism, however, assumes — as McManus repeatedly notes, citing J.S. Mill, Rawls, Marx, Macpherson, Rosselli, Wollstonecraft, Paine and others — that, simultaneously, the liberal project must be defended from left-wing critiques and the socialist project from liberal critiques. As the brilliant Carlo Rosselli, an early proponent of liberal socialism, once put it:

> Socialism is nothing more than the logical development, taken to its extreme consequences, of the principle of liberty. Socialism, when understood in its fundamental sense and judged by its results — as the concrete movement for the emancipation of the proletariat — is liberalism in action; it means that liberty comes into the life of poor people.[3]

In short: the liberal and socialist viewpoints should be understood less as inherently contradictory and more as existing in a relationship of mutual dependence. The full

---

2   Cf. McManus, 2025, 2ff.

3   Cf. Carlo Rosselli and Nadia Urbinati, ed. *Liberal Socialism*, 2017, 86.

realization of the liberal project's commitment to freedom is contingent upon the establishment of social (i.e., institutional and economic) frameworks that empower individuals to actively exercise their autonomy by participating as active agents in shaping their own lives — a connection that McManus rightly emphasizes, noting the unique interrelation of *methodological-collectivist* and *normative-individualist* dimensions within the liberal socialist project.[4]

Finally, I would like to comment on this book's title: *What is Liberal Socialism?* While McManus' recent book was titled *The Political Theory of Liberal Socialism*, the title of this book implicitly points to a characteristic feature of the liberal socialist project: the absence of a definitive answer. The strength of this theory lies, paradoxically, in its ambiguity. Liberal socialism can be understood as a project defined by openness, plurality and contingent developments. The heterogeneity of intellectual approaches to liberal socialism — as McManus' elucidates with clarity and presents uniquely in this important book — underscores this aspect.

I would like to conclude these remarks by invoking Raymond Geuss's observation that "liberalism is in the intended sense an amorphous and shifting collection of things with a clear ability to renew itself, change its shape and revise the formulation of its central beliefs."[5] In other words, a key (theoretical and normative) element of the foundational liberal idea is its capacity for change. The essays collected in this book clearly demonstrate that this process of change, if one follows the basic normative premises of the liberal idea to their logical conclusion, can

---

4   Cf. McManus, 2025, 17–18.
5   Cf. Raymond Geuss, *Not Thinking Like a Liberal*, 2022, 7_8. https://www.hup.harvard.edu/books/9780674270343

culminate in a reformulation of the socialist idea. In short: in a liberal socialism.

Florian Maiwald
Bonn, 24th of April

INTRODUCTION

Socialism is nothing more than the logical development, taken to its extreme consequences, of the principle of liberty. Socialism, when understood in its fundamental sense and judged by its results — as the concrete movement for the emancipation of the proletariat — is liberalism in action; it means that liberty comes into the life of poor people. Socialism says the abstract recognition of liberty of conscience and political freedoms for all, though it may represent an essential moment in the development of political theory, is a thing of very limited value when the majority of men, forced to live as a result of circumstances of birth and environment in moral and material poverty, are left without the possibility of appreciating its significance and taking any actual advantage of it. Liberty without the accompaniment and support of a minimum of economic autonomy, without emancipation from the grip of pressing material necessity, does not exist for the individual; it is a mere phantasm.

Carlo Rosselli, Liberal Socialism

The articles in this collection were written during a decade of crisis for liberalism, as it became increasingly clear that the era of neoliberal "end of history" was coming to an end after 25 years, give or take. Few will mourn it, and fewer should. Neoliberalism has proven as uninspired in practice as many Leftists recognized it was in theory: an apologia for capitalism so unqualified it affirmed the most vulgar of vulgar Marxist stereotypes about liberalism as the hand-maiden ideology of capital.

One of the major reasons for the failures of neoliberalism was its loss of any futural sensibility. The time consciousness of the neoliberal era was invariably phenomenological rather than historical. Its lifeworld was characterized by the extension of an ethic of commodification into all cultural spheres, eventually even interpellating neoliberal subjects themselves. We became "a brand called you" — apprehending others and ourselves according to the competitive logic of the market. Over time the alienation and loss of identity this induced contributed to the rise of post-modern conservatism and fascism as distinctly twenty-first-century forms of reaction. Like many earlier forms of reactionary politics, these both rejected and assimilated many of the characteristics of what they reacted against. Post-modern Rightists rejected the "liberal" features of neoliberalism, while hardening its competitive ethos and extending them to new subjects by rejuvenating discourses about race, IQ, gender and sexual identity. For many on the Right the competitive stratification induced by neoliberal culture required us to be more ruthless and less empathetic in our concern for others. Whether this meant doubling down on pseudo-Nietzschean emphases on individual greatness by elevating the tech bros or adopting a more solidaristic form of ethnocentrism predicated on racial social Darwinism remains an open question on the Right. What isn't an open question is the right's sense that the future is theirs.

Except that it is not, in fact, a future. These forms of reactionary politics compound and radicalize the worst impulses of the neoliberal era rather than challenge them. It may be easier to imagine the end of the world than Elon Musk getting us to Mars. But it is harder than ever to think through a plausible alternative to capitalism we can vest our hopes in, and it is this very sense of hopelessness that contributes to the nihilistic appeal of reactionary politics.

Liberal socialism is, at its core, a philosophy of hope. Unlike the "radical" Right, it is in fact a radical doctrine. In the oldest sense of the word, liberal socialism critiques a staid liberal status quo because it wishes to get to the root of its crisis and generate new and healthier growth. Liberal socialists have long recognized that liberalism is at its strongest as a fighting, future-oriented creed that seeks to make real the promise of liberty, equality and solidarity in the lives of all. Including the working classes, poor women, colonized subjects and more for whom liberalism has always been at best a promise and at worst a promise broken.

Liberal socialism is not a monolith. As the essays in this collection make clear, many of its most insightful figures differed greatly on theoretical and practical issues. Charles Mills had little patience for John Rawls' philosophical removal from concrete problems of race and empire. Mary Wollstonecraft would have little patience for the lingering misogyny of class reductionism. Liberal socialism is also far from a perfect tradition. As I argue in *The Political Theory of Liberal Socialism,* any "retrieval" of this theoretical tradition needs to recognize its considerable failures. These range from J.S Mill's unforgiveable defense of imperialism to Rosselli's heroic defeat n the face of fascist tyranny. This collection of essays shouldn't be construed as a fully systematic defense of my own version of liberal socialism. It is a popularization of the tradition. But any liberal socialism in the twenty-first century will need to be considerably wiser and savvier if it is to have a chance at being instituted. This will invariably mean learning far more from the rich Marxist tradition of theorizing on power and imperialism than liberal socialists have been willing to do in the past.

My own hypothesis is that, at the theoretical level, a synthesis of Marx and Rawls is the way forward. This might appear an unusual combination given that Marx was a dialectical and historical materialist whose great accomplishment was the critique of capitalist political economy rather than writing recipe books for the cook shops of the future. By contrast Rawls is *the* ideal theoretical philosopher par excellence — conceiving hypothetical normative contracts than engender general principles of justice to be applied to the basic structure of society. But scratch beneath the surface and there are theoretical joints where the two can be combined. One is of course Rawls' own acknowledgment in both the *Lectures on the History of Political Philosophy* and *Lectures on the History of Moral Philosophy* that "justice as fairness" owes a deep debt to Hegel and Marx. This ranges from taking the basic structure, rather than the individual and her rights, as the chief subject of justice, to Rawls calling for liberal socialism or "property owning democracy" in *Justice as Fairness: A Restatement.*

At a deeper level, Marx and Rawls both draw heavily on the tradition of German idealism that still constitutes the deepest thinking on social and political problems in the Western canon. In particular, Marx recognizes from at least the *Grundrisse* on that the point of a critique of political economy isn't to just be crudely critical of capitalist arguments. Instead it is to show how material and historical contexts generate the conditions under which the laws of capitalist political economy emerge, which are in turn cognized and reified by political economists. The "critique" of political economy is intended to show the generative limitations of both our ways of apprehending capitalism and its real, material limitations as a mode of production. This is of course a project Rawls would recognize as a profound rethinking of Kant and Hegel. In this sense, Marx's project enjoys genealogical kinship epistemologically and transcendentally with what "justice as fairness" achieves at a normative level. A key insight of Rawlsian theory is the need to never naturalize or reify social inequalities, treating them as immutable facts about the world which we simply must bear. As Rawls notes in *Theory of Justice*, facts about the differences between human beings are just that. What normatively matters is how social institutions respond to these facts. Here, any just liberal socialist society would have a lot of work to do.

These extremely provisional remarks about a potential Rawlsian-Marxist defense of liberal socialism are not intended as an argument but a suggestion. None of the essays in *What is Liberal Socialism?*, whether written by myself or the great Florian Maiwald and Paul Crider, are intended to be a final word. Our hope in this collection is simply to broaden the possibility of liberal socialism to a potentially skeptical Leftist audience in a spirit of good faith. And to do so in a way that is a little more accessible and digestible than a long academic monograph like *The Political Theory of Liberal Socialism*. Should readers be intrigued by liberal socialism but dissatisfied with the presentation here, we'd be delighted if they gave their own unique spin on the tradition. After all, liberal socialism shares with both liberalism and democratic socialism an appreciation for rich pluralism and debate.

The answer to the question "What is liberal socialism?" will therefore hopefully be a provisional one. Our hope is that our readers will treat this book like a ladder to be discarded once they've come up with a higher answer by themselves.

Solidarity.

Matt McManus,
Spring 2025

Part I: What Is Liberal Socialism?

LIBERAL SOCIALISM NOW![1]

Very few of us expected liberalism to have such a rocky twenty-first century. At the turn of the twentieth, liberal ideology and liberal democratic political institutions seemed more legitimate and secure than ever before. Liberals had defeated their great geopolitical rivals on the fascist Right and the communist Left. How things change.

Over the past few decades, discontent and disdain for liberalism have spread across huge swathes of the globe, led by a resurgent Right-wing populism that denounced its materialism, universalism and libertine decadence. Wannabe strongmen like Victor Orban declared they were constructing new kinds of 'illiberal democracy' — a half truth, since the regimes would be illiberal, but not particularly democratic. Books flooded the market with alarmist or triumphalist titles such as *Why Liberalism Failed* (2018) or *A World After Liberalism* (2021), all of which diagnosed its failures with relish or fear. Theories about what had gone wrong multiplied. Liberalism was too atomistic, too alienating, too antidemocratic, too democratic for its own good, too beholden to the ignorant masses, too elitist, even too boring and politically correct for its own good.

---

1   Originally Printed in *Aeon Magazine*.

What was often lost in the discourse around liberalism in the twenty-first century was whether it could simultaneously be worth saving while also having deserved the ignominy into which it was falling. From the 1970s onward, many liberal politicians and theorists had backed away from the more progressive and transformative propensities of the tradition. The era of big liberal dreams about establishing a "great" or "just" society was over.

Internalizing a host of conservative arguments, liberals like Isaiah Berlin or Friedrich Hayek argued that big dreams were dangerous and contrary to liberalism, its revolutionary past aside. The best one could hope for was a competitive and highly inequitable neoliberal society defined by ordered liberty and at most a minimal welfare state. That such a consciously deflated vision became associated with technocratic aloofness, a lack of principled conviction and a wariness of democratic accountability came as a surprise only to neoliberals *circa* 2016. More thoughtful commentators followed Samuel Moyn's claim in *Liberalism Against Itself* (2023) that if liberals couldn't rediscover how to not just fearmonger but inspire, they were unlikely to see their doctrine survive much longer and, "anyway, survival is not good enough."

Moyn is right that, if liberals trade off presenting an inspiring vision of the future for mere survival, they are unlikely to get either. The existential woes of twenty-first-century liberalism require we do more than return to the forms of neoliberal governance that generated discontent in the first place. It requires retrieving the revolutionary emancipatory and egalitarian ethos that defined liberalism at its revolutionary best to offer a new deal to citizens of liberal states. The strand of liberal political theory that offers the richest guidance on what form this new deal should take is liberal socialism.

The idea of "liberal socialism" might appear odd and even oxymoronic. This is especially true for those on the Right and the Left who regard liberalism as the philosophy of market capitalism. Of course, there are many classical and neoliberal thinkers for whom that is true. From John Locke's emphatic defence of life, liberty and property to Hayek's declaration that state planning in the economy was the road to serfdom, liberal defences of the ethics of capitalism are easy to find. The economist Ludwig von Mises no doubt spoke for many (including plenty on the Left) when, in his polemical tract *Liberalism* (1927), he proudly declared that:

> the programme of liberalism... if condensed into a single word, would have to read: *property*, that is, private ownership of the means of production... All the other demands of liberalism result from this fundamental demand.

But this would be to ignore the reality that many great liberal thinkers have historically been wary (to downright critical) of capitalism. This goes far back. Adam Smith may have been an enthusiast for free trade and market liberties, but in *The Theory of Moral Sentiments* (1759) he also decried how:

> this disposition to admire, and almost to worship, the rich and the powerful, and to despise, or, at least, to neglect persons of poor and mean condition, though necessary both to establish and to maintain the distinction of ranks and the order of society, is, at the same time, the great and most universal cause of the corruption of our moral sentiments.

This was reiterated in Smith's polemics against monopolization and the alienating effects of the division of labour in *The Wealth of Nations* (1776). By the industrial era, some of the greatest liberal thinkers expressed sympathy and even came to align themselves with socialism. John Stuart Mill, the greatest liberal philosopher of the nineteenth century, openly declared himself a socialist in his *Autobiography* (1873) and stressed in *Socialism* (1879) how "great poverty, and that poverty very little connected with desert — are the first grand failure of the existing arrangements of society."

Mill was hardly alone in sympathizing with such a fusion of liberalism and socialism. In his essay collection *Democratic Theory: Essays in Retrieval* (1973), the political theorist C.B. Macpherson coined the term "retrieval" to refer to getting "clear of the disabling central defect of current liberal-democratic theory, while holding on to, or recovering, the humanistic values which liberal democracy has always claimed." We must now make an effort to retrieve the political theory of liberal socialism and make the case for its salience in the twenty-first century (a project I continue in *The Political Theory of Liberal Socialism*).

Liberal socialism is a political ideology that combines support for many liberal political institutions and rights with a socialist desire to establish far more equitable and democratic economic arrangements. The latter point is put plainly by Michael Walzer in his book *The Struggle for a Decent Politics* (2023), in which he writes that, "while liberal socialists are not 'egalitarianist,l' they are serious about equality — more so, generally, than liberal democrats." This deeper concern for equality relative to classical liberals becomes apparent when we look at when liberal socialism emerged and how its major figures defended its core arguments.

There is extensive debate over periodizing classical liberal theory. Many date its origins to the seventeenth century and the writings of Locke, Baruch Spinoza and Hugo

Grotius among others. Whether or not these thinkers can be correctly labelled "liberals" full stop, they undoubtedly developed or systematized a lot of the theoretical architecture that later liberals would rely on. By contrast, in *Liberalism* (2nd ed., 2014) Edmund Fawcett insists that mature liberal political philosophy only really appeared on the scene in the nineteenth century, when the term itself became popularized and self-described 'liberal' parties and movements began to appear.

Whoever you agree with, there's no doubt that liberal socialism emerged later than classical liberalism, extending the latter's antipathy to the hierarchical *ancien régimes* of Europe to demand more radical changes still. While mature forms of liberal socialist political theory didn't appear until the mid-nineteenthth century, there were important precursor figures. Two of the most influential predecessors to liberal socialism were Thomas Paine and Mary Wollstonecraft.

Paine remains most famous for his stirring rhetorical defences of the American and French revolutions and his acidic polemics against Edmund Burke and conservatism in *Rights of Man* (1791). Until recently, Paine was largely viewed as an extraordinary pamphleteer for the classical liberal and republican viewpoint, while not being an especially original thinker or theorist. That appraisal has since undergone a major shift, with Robert Lamb in 2015 stressing Paine's importance as a theorist whose 'every instinct' was egalitarian.[2]

Paine is an important precursor to liberal socialism because he embraced the importance of individual flourishing and rights, while becoming increasingly sceptical that this

---

2   Robert Lamb, *Thomas Paine and the Idea of Human Rights*, Cambridge, 2015.

could be achieved without a major redistribution of wealth and privilege. In the pamphlet "Agrarian Justice" (1797), he rejects the methodological individualism of classical liberal approaches to property rights, and insists that property is an eminently social phenomenon:

> Personal property is the effect of society; and it is as impossible for an individual to acquire personal property without the aid of society, as it is for him to make land originally. Separate an individual from society, and give him an island or continent to possess, and he cannot acquire personal property.

He goes on to suggest that, since many wealthy people monopolize productive land and capital without giving anything back, they owe a major debt to the poor as a matter of right. In the second part of the *Rights of Man* and in "Agrarian Justice," Paine develops these arguments into a call for redistribution, sketching out an early scheme for the welfare state. This includes providing money for education, guaranteed employment for those who want it, a stipend for every child born and a prototype of an old-age pension.

Wollstonecraft was less policy-minded than her contemporary Paine, but even more scathing in her contempt for the corrosive effect of the inequities of property that defined aristocratic and early capitalist societies. In her classic *A Vindication of the Rights of Woman* (1792), Wollstonecraft insisted that:

> From the respect paid to property flow, as from a poisoned fountain, most of the evils and vices which render this world such a dreary scene to the contemplative mind. For it is in the most polished society that noisome reptiles and venomous serpents lurk under the rank herbage; and there is voluptuousness pampered by the still sultry air, which

relaxes every good disposition before it ripens into virtue. One class presses on another; for all are aiming to procure respect on account of their property: and property, once gained, will procure the respect due only to talents and virtue.

In her later *Letters Written During a Short Residence in Sweden, Norway and Denmark* (1796), she lambasts the nouveaux riches as a "fungus" with the criticism that:

An ostentatious display of wealth without elegance, and a greedy enjoyment of pleasure without sentiment, embrutes them till they term all virtue of a heroic cast, romantic attempts at something above our nature, and anxiety about the welfare of others, a search after misery in which we have no concern.

Wollstonecraft believed in private property, arguing it was a just reward for labour. But even this had a radical connotation, as she was critical of those who lived in luxury or defended privilege while ignoring the "women who gained a livelihood by selling vegetables or fish, who never had had any advantages of education..." Her critique of the idle or undeserving rich both echoes Locke's condemnation of aristocracy and anticipates later Ricardian socialist and Marxist condemnations of the parasitic wealthy.

Much like Paine, Wollstonecraft had an unfailingly egalitarian instinct (including, of course, on gender relations) insisting there "must be more equality established in society, or morality will never gain ground..." In her ideal society there would be neither rich nor poor, and the competitive race to accumulate private property would be a far less significant social priority than the relatively equal development of human intellectual, artistic and moral powers. It's this solidaristic emphasis on the development of human powers in a society of equals that makes Wollstonecraft such an important figure in the movement toward liberal socialism.

Liberal socialism reached its maturity in the nineteenth century with John Stuart Mill, its most articulate and well-known spokesman. Early in his career, Mill had been a more conventional supporter of the free market. But, later in life, mostly under the influence of the utopian socialist St Simonians, he shifted his views markedly. In his *Autobiography*, Mill declared that his "ideal of ultimate improvement went far beyond Democracy, and would class us decidedly under the general designation of Socialists." While being critical of statist forms of socialism and expressing a wariness of the threat they posed to liberty, he claimed to look "forward to a time when society will no longer be divided into the idle and the industrious; when the rule that they who do not work shall not eat, will be applied not to paupers only, but impartially to all."

This shift toward socialism was reflected in later editions of the *Principles of Political Economy* (1848). Mill defended extensive experiments with workplace democracy and co-operatives, arguing that they would potentially be less domineering, more economically efficient and more conducive to the flourishing of workers. As Helen McCabe traces in her excellent book *John Stuart Mill: Socialist* (2021), he also came to advocate for wealth redistribution through:

> state ownership of railways and roads, and municipal ownership (and provision) of utilities such as gas and water. He also at least suggested it would be permissible for the government to provide public hospitals; national banks; a postal service; 'manufactories'; and a corps of civil engineers, so long as the government did not maintain a monopoly on these professions or services.

Mill's flavour of liberal socialism based around co-operatives and a generous welfare state anticipated many contemporary forms of market socialism, as well as being a direct inspiration to important ethical and Christian socialists such as R.H. Tawney.

In the early to mid-twentieth century, an impressive array of authors came to endorse liberal socialism. In a 1939 interview with *The New Statesman and Nation*, John Maynard Keynes proposed:

> [A move out of the] nineteenth-century laissez-faire state into an era of liberal socialism … where we can act as an organised community for common purposes and to promote economic and social justice, whilst respecting and protecting the individual — his freedom of choice, his faith, his mind and its expression, his enterprise and his property.

A variety of European democratic socialists such as Eduard Bernstein and Carlo Rosselli worked to theorize closer connections between liberalism and socialism, echoing Mill's claim that socialists were the more "far-sighted successors" of liberalism. Bernstein's classic *The Preconditions of Socialism* (1899) offered a sustained critique of orthodox Marxist revolutionary theory and proposed a conciliation with liberalism. He insisted that "with respect to liberalism as a historical movement, socialism is its legitimate heir, not only chronologically, but also intellectually," and stressed that there is "no liberal thought that is not also part of the intellectual equipment of socialism." Rosselli made similar claims in his book *Liberal Socialism* (1930), holding that:

> Socialism is nothing more than the logical development, taken to its extreme consequences, of the principle of liberty. Socialism, when understood in its fundamental sense

and judged by its results — as the concrete movement for the emancipation of the proletariat — is liberalism in action; it means that liberty comes into the life of poor people.

While he never identified with the label, I'd argue that Macpherson can also be correctly characterized as a liberal socialist, given his lifelong effort to "retrieve" a radical democratic and egalitarian core to the liberal tradition.

Finally, in the United States John Dewey worked hard to extend American conceptions of democracy beyond the horizon of the state. His most famous contributions were of course in education, where Dewey insisted on the pedagogical superiority a more egalitarian classroom where students actively participated in their learning rather than being regarded as passive recipients of knowledge delivered by an intellectual superior. But Dewey was also keen to extend democratic principles to the workplace, becoming president of the League for Industrial Democracy in 1939 and advocating for the labour movement.

In the postwar era, there have been several prominent figures aligned with liberal socialism, including Irving Howe, Michael Walzer and Chantal Mouffe. But by far the most significant figure to express sympathy for liberal socialism was John Rawls. For a long time, Rawls's brick-like *Theory of Justice* (1971) was taken as an apologia for the welfare state system that, tragically, began to decline right about when the book was published. But this understates Rawls's radicalism. In his *Lectures on the History of Political Philosophy* (2000), Rawls described Karl Marx as "heroic" and praised his "marvellous" intellectual gifts. By the time of his swan song, *Justice as Fairness: A Restatement* (2001), Rawls insisted that welfarism did not do a good enough job of realizing liberal principles of justice. Only a property-owning democracy or "liberal socialism" would be sufficient. While Rawls himself wrote more about property-owning democracy, Edmundson's book *John Rawls: Reticent Socialist* (2017) makes a powerful case for why the most rigorous interpretation of justice as fairness would require liberal socialism instead.

As history shows, liberal socialists are not a monolith. They disagree on many core points. Some of these are theoretical: Is the strongest basis for liberal socialism some kind of utilitarianism, deontology or pragmatism? Other divides are over practical questions such as the relationship between statist welfarism and bottom-up democratization of the economy; Mill famously vested his hopes in worker co-ops where many modern liberal socialists focus on social programmes. Nevertheless, all liberal socialists are committed to three central principles, which I've arranged from the more abstract to the more concrete.

First, liberal socialists are committed to methodological collectivism and normative individualism. They believe that the wellbeing and free development of individual persons (and, for a growing number, nonhuman animals) is the highest moral priority. However, they disagree with many classical liberals' insular and competitive conception of human nature and their individualist approach to conceiving social relations.[3] Liberal socialists hold that, to properly think through how individuals will best thrive, one must recognize their embeddedness in society and how it can improve or disrupt their capacity to lead a good life.

Secondly, liberal socialists are committed to each person having as equal an opportunity to lead as good a life as possible through the provision of shared resources for the development and expression of their human powers. To put it another way, liberal socialists focus on the free development of human powers or capabilities along a wide

---

3   Tony Smith, *Beyond Liberal Egalitarianism*, Haymarket, 2018.

array of metrics. What Macpherson calls a "developmental ethic" can be contrasted with the extractive and possessive ethic characteristic of classical liberalism and hedonistic forms of utilitarianism. Where the extractive/possessive ethic holds that the good life comes from production and consumption, the developmental ethic of liberal socialism emphasizes the equal development and application of each individual's powers as a condition for their flourishing.

Thirdly, liberal socialists believe in a highly participatory liberal democratic regime that extends liberal rights and democracy into the economy. This does not include a right to private ownership of the means of production. While all liberal socialists believe in rights to personal property, this doesn't extend to rights to acquire forms of property that would enable forms of workplace domination or political plutocracy to develop. In these instances, what impacts all should, in part, be decided upon by all.

Liberal socialist authors will defend and articulate these principles in various idioms, and emphasize one or another to various degrees. This testifies to the internal diversity of the tradition, if nothing else. Macpherson was very critical of atomistic "possessive individualism" but supported a liberal humanist ethic of developing people's capacities or powers. Nevertheless, he had comparatively little to say about what kind of social structure could realize this ethic. In *The Socialist Decision* (1933), Paul Tillich offers a theological defence of liberal democratic socialism, which obviously runs counter to the secular approaches of Mill and Rawls. Mouffe's agonistic liberal socialism foregrounds[4] the importance of political contestation far more than Rawls's temperate insistence that a pluralistic society needs to unite around an "overlapping consensus." Charles

---

4   Chantal Mouffe, "Toward a Liberal Socialism," *Dissent*, Winter 1993.

Mill's "black radical liberalism" rightly takes many Left-liberals to task for ignoring, or even supporting, imperialism and racism.[5] But behind this variety is a core conviction that taking seriously commitments to liberty, equality and solidarity requires going beyond the social hierarchies established under capitalism.

Given the eminence of many of the figures attracted to liberal socialism, it is somewhat perplexing that the term can seem oxymoronic. The explanation probably has more to do with politics than philosophy, especially in the US. As Moyn points out in *Liberalism Against Itself*, throughout the mid-twentieth century, many prominent "Cold War liberals" turned against the more progressive and egalitarian elements in the tradition. This led to the banishing of Jean-Jacques Rousseau, G.W.F. Hegel and Marx to the fringes, and the dilution of the more radical arguments of prominent liberals like Mill. By the time liberal egalitarians began to marshal formidable theoretical arguments for welfarism and social democracy in the 1970s, the opportunity to realize such an agenda had passed. Neoliberalism had taken hold across much of the world, further squeezing out progressive forms of liberalism and liberal socialism.

Nevertheless, the future for liberal socialist political theory is bright. While not everyone listed below would identify with the label (and some might reject it), a considerable number of prominent and up-and-coming theorists have been working to bring out the affinities between the two traditions and canonize (or re-canonize) the major figures. These include Helen McCabe, Michael Walzer, James Crotty, Chantal Mouffe, Igor Shoikhedbrod,

---

5   Charles W. Mills, "Epilogue (as Prologue): Toward a Black Radical Liberalism," in Charles W. Mills, ed., *Black Rights/White Wrongs*, Oxford, 2017.

Lillian Cicerchia, Samuel Moyn, Daniel Chandler, William Edmundson, Elizabeth Anderson, Tony Smith, Rodney Peffer and and increasingly popular politicians like AOC, Zohran Mamdani and others.

It isn't hard to see why the prospect of liberal socialism would be appealing today. Liberalism remains in or near crisis, and vast numbers express discontent with the neo-liberal status quo. At the same time, there are very good reasons to reject revisiting forms of authoritarian "real existing socialism" and communism. Liberal socialism offers the prospect of combining respect for liberal rights, checks and balances on state power and participatory democracy with socialist concerns for the equal flourishing of all in a sustainable environment, the extension of democratic concerns into the workplace and "private government," and pushing back on plutocratic rule. It also philosophically aligns well with concrete democratic socialist and radical movements appearing in the US, Chile, Brazil and elsewhere that want radical economic change but align with liberal values. Whether liberal socialism can transition from being a theoretical tradition and become a popular political ideology is a hard question. But, in a world defined by growing anger at inequality and plutocracy, liberal socialism is worthy of our loyalty.

WHY SOCIALISTS SHOULDN'T REJECT LIBERALISM[1]

For many socialists, liberalism is at best a kind of bourgeois conformism and at worst an outright reactionary doctrine. For centuries now, socialists have developed probing criticisms of liberalism — too atomistic, too unequal, too imperialist — and looked forward to the day when it would be overcome and replaced by a higher form of society.

At the same time, even as hardened a critic as Karl Marx offered a far more sophisticated and generous critique of liberalism than is sometimes admitted. Even in the nineteenth century, it was clear that classical liberalism was a significant advance on the old feudal order. Since then, many liberals have taken on board the most serious Left critiques and tried to show how liberal democracy is not only compatible with but may even require a commitment to economic democratization and equality.

These themes are explored at length in Matt McManus's intriguing book, *The Political Theory of Liberal Socialism*, Political scientist Igor Shoikhedbrod spoke with McManus about the book. McManus argues that while liberalism has

---

1   Interview with Igor Shoikhedbrod reprinted from *Jacobin Magazine.*

its flaws, socialists should not be too quick to dispense with liberal ideas entirely.

Igor Shoikhedbrod

What motivated you to pursue the political theory of liberal socialism?

Matt McManus

There were a few motivations going all the way back to my early political and intellectual interests. Probably the most important were agonistic.

Firstly, the political Right has made major gains around much of the world. It's hard to say whether its high-water mark has been reached but in 2018 it dominated the United States, Brazil, India, Russia and many other countries. This inspired a lot of thinking about how to coalesce in opposition to the Right.

Second, and relatedly, I spent the better part of the past decade reading a great deal about the Right and its main intellectual currents. There is a crude, visceral kind of right-wing rhetoric that just conflates anything to the left of Ronald Reagan together — think about all these books on "race Marxism" — that see woke capitalism and liberal centrism as the second coming of [Vladimir] Lenin. But all that time reading the Right did convince me that philosophers like [Friedrich] Nietzsche and [Martin] Heidegger are correct that there are deep metaphysical affinities between liberal and socialist humanism.

To the extent that liberalism and socialism are committed to reason, humanism and securing a good life for all, the affinity is to be embraced.

In *Introduction to Metaphysics*, Heidegger dismisses liberalism and socialism as "metaphysically the same" in their inauthentic embrace of modernity and humanism. I think there's truth to this, except I don't share Heidegger's gloomy conclusions. To the extent that liberalism and socialism are committed to reason, humanism and securing a good life for all, the affinity is to be embraced.

Finally, I've always felt that Leftists had more sympathy for elements of liberalism than they let on. If you ask the average Leftist if they believe in freedom of religion, mobility, voting rights or expression, they'll say yes. If anything, they'll insist those achievements are not safe in the hands of normie liberals. So *The Political Theory of Liberal Socialism* is in part an effort to make explicit those shared commitments.

I.S.

What are the differences between liberal socialism and social democracy, between liberal socialism and democratic socialism?

M.M.

I think it makes more sense to see these "differences" as a continuum rather than a categorical either/or. If anything, it's undialectical to conceptualize different social forms in these stark ways while not recognizing the links between them — something I took from your book, actually, when you mention how Marx insists any new socialist society will be "stamped" by features of the old.

Understood as a matter of accentuation and qualitative rather than categorical distinction, a core difference with social democracy is the extent to which relations of production remained largely unchanged in many countries. Workers still largely labored for capitalists in a wage labor system, even if some valuable efforts were made to induce greater unionization or introduce codetermination mechanisms. What did change was the extent to which the state intervened to regulate the economy and redistribute wealth through social programs like the National Health Service in Britain or Social Security in the United States.

By contrast, a liberal socialist regime would have to place far more emphasis on implementing Left-liberal principles in the workplace. This will mean extending liberal rights there to offset the power of bosses. But it will also mean very substantially democratizing power to eliminate the domination of what Elizabeth Anderson calls "private government." Codetermination and unionization are good starts here, but very much just a beginning. This can be accompanied by far more substantial redistributions of wealth with the aim of not just catering to people's needs but ensuring they get fair value from their political liberties as equal citizens.

I.S.

Karl Marx once referred to J.S. Mill as a "shallow syncretist" bent on "reconciling irreconcilables." How would you respond to the same charges against the project of "liberal socialism" as you understand it?

M.M.

Marx's critique to a certain extent overshoots its target. He's obviously absolutely correct that you cannot just change the distribution of surplus wealth however you want without also fundamentally transforming relations of production. To your earlier question, this was a core problem in many social democratic states where redistribution could temporarily reach relatively generous levels. But much of that fell apart because the power of capital resurged, which contributed to the neoliberal counterattack, as David Harvey explains.

But Mill was in many ways much less indifferent to this problem than Marx was aware of, and the same is true of many other liberal socialists. Mill's call for workplace co-operatives was intended as part of a campaign to eventually do away with capitalists and was to be accompanied by economic redistribution and education programs to help bring about political equality. And of course, Mill was more farsighted than Marx on the need to secure rights for women, even if he was less admirable on questions like British imperialism.

Finally, it's not obvious to me that we should always take the most uncompromising Marxist's side in their debate with Left-liberals like Mill. Marx himself was a radically democratic thinker, but the way some Marxists simply dismissed important liberal ideas like checks and balances on state power or individual rights against the state would of course have a dark legacy. Mill was in some ways prophetic in warning socialists about the danger of such dismissals, and contemporary socialists don't want to fall into the same trap as some of our forebears.

I.S.
At what point does liberalism conflict with socialism and vice versa? In other words, what are the boundary lines between liberalism and socialism?

M.M.
I think we need to be careful here to recognize that liberalism is really a family of liberalisms, and the same is true of socialism. Whether liberalism and socialism harmonize and reinforce each other or conflict depends in part on which members of the respective families you put together.

Socialists have rightly been very critical of the atomistic egoism of what C.B. Macpherson calls classical liberal "possessive individualism" and its ethic of endless acquisition. Socialists foregrounded how it is destructive of solidarity and community. Contemporaneously we've seen possessive strains of liberalism carry on within the neoliberal or "Cold War liberal" traditions, which have proven as uninspired in practice as they were uninspiring in theory. The high levels of inequalities and power led many to rightly feel that governments had no interest in ordinary people and their needs, which opened the door for figures like [Donald] Trump to mobilize those resentments, even if he doubled down on many of the worst policies in office.

But there are other forms of liberalism going back to Thomas Paine which were also critical of atomistic individualism and the ethic of endless acquisition. Paine was one of the first to call for the foundation of a welfare state, and he justified it by pointing out that property was a social institution, meaning the rich owed society a debt for their riches. Black radical liberals like Charles Mills have shown how we can begin (and it will be a long process) to divest liberalism, and for that matter many strands of socialism, of their racial and racist assumptions and move in a more genuinely egalitarian direction. These forms of liberalism are very much compatible with many forms of socialism, at least those many forms of socialism that are hostile to authoritarian states and command economies.

I.S.
What, if anything, does liberalism add to socialism? What, if anything, does socialism add to liberalism?

M.M.
Liberalism in many ways anteceded socialism as the great modernist doctrine committed to liberty, equality and solidarity for all. The ideas have roots that go back deeper still, but the liberal tradition deserves praise for raising them to revolutionary potential, as any good Marxist would point

out. I think today one of the core things it adds to socialism is the need to protect individual rights and impose significant limitations on state power.

Deeper than that, one can stress how liberalism contributes a much-needed sense of anti-utopianism to the socialist tradition. Some socialists assumed the state would wither away once the capacity to meet everyone's needs was met. Many even thought socialism would perfect human nature. As Leon Trotsky once put it:

The shell in which the cultural construction and self-education of Communist man will be enclosed, will develop all the vital elements of contemporary art to the highest point. Man will become immeasurably stronger, wiser and subtler; his body will become more harmonized, his movements more rhythmic, his voice more musical. The forms of life will become dynamically dramatic. The average human type will rise to the heights of an Aristotle, a Goethe, or a Marx. And above this ridge new peaks will rise.

I don't think that's really plausible.

Indeed, a core insight of liberalism that can marry quite easily to socialism is that human beings might ethically and cognitively improve, but they will never be perfected and many of our most sinister features will persist as long as we do. Call it the Augustinian principle. In fact, I'd follow Ben Burgis in maintaining that a core argument for socialism should be a wariness of human nature and how easily it can be corrupted when some people enjoy enormous amounts of power and wealth.

What liberals need to learn from socialists is the importance of hope and to rediscover this commitment to ethical and cognitive improvement. Samuel Moyn wrote a great book, *Liberalism Against Itself*, that was a big influence on me. He points out how many of the Cold War liberals nipped a productive dialogue between liberalism and socialism in the bud. They insisted that any attempt to improve the world was dangerous and opened the door to authoritarianism. And they were especially concerned about granting the masses too much power. Well, it turns out their anxieties were misplaced; the door to authoritarianism opens when liberals don't offer ordinary people the hope that suffuses socialism.

On top of that, liberals can learn from socialists how dangerous economic concentrations of wealth are, since they readily turn into concentrations of power. This is a lesson Marx taught long ago, and liberals have forgotten and had to relearn generation after generation.

I. S.

How do you account for the largely dismal track record of political alliances between liberals and the radical Left, including socialists?

M.M.

Theoretically, I think there are a lot of us, going back some time, who have wanted to put the two together. The term "liberal socialism" isn't unique to me. In the book, I claim Mill was the first "mature" liberal socialist, even if he didn't use the term, but others like [Carlo] Rosselli and [John] Rawls explicitly used it well before I got to it.

Practically the difficulties are a lot more stark. Socialists and liberals managed a workable alliance in the face of the fascist Right during World War II, and we're much the better for it. Beyond those kinds of existentially pitched circumstances, it is difficult. Many liberals would agree with Ludwig von Mises that the core commitment of liberalism is to private property, and obviously socialists can have no truck with that. My response is that if liberalism really can be boiled down to little more than a fetish for property, it isn't an inspiring credo worth allying with.

If liberalism really can be boiled down to little more than a fetish for property, it isn't an inspiring credo worth allying with.

But I don't think that's true of many liberals. For plenty of people who identify with the label today, liberalism is about securing something like a dignified life for everyone, regardless of their circumstances. The goal of socialists should be to hold a mirror up to liberals and say that they cannot achieve their goals unless they're willing to extend liberal principles about equality and freedom from domination to the economy.

I.S.

What arguments can you provide for a renewed alliance between the two traditions today, particularly for those who think that "liberal socialism" is a contradiction in terms

M.M.

Liberalism and socialism are linked historically, morally and many would say spiritually to the great struggles for emancipation that reshaped the world between the seventeenth and twentieth centuries. At their best, both are revolutionary and forward-looking doctrines that reject the Right's claims that there are superior persons in society who are entitled to more, and insist that it is as important that a poor single mother's life goes as well as Elon Musk's. That we don't live in such a society is the fault of unjust social arrangements that can be changed for the better and must be.

If liberals don't learn from socialists and vice versa, we might not see either doctrine survive into the twenty-first century. But if they do, liberalism and socialism will deserve more than survival: they'll deserve loyalty and even love.

THE BEST OF LIBERALISM POINTS TO SOCIALISM[1]

Enzo Rossi recently published a provocative essay, "Socialism is Not Liberal Moralism on Steroids", for *Damage*.[2] In it, Rossi argues against "left-liberals" and "self-described liberal socialists," both of which he associates with "social democracy" — a "short lived anomaly in the history of capitalism." Rossi takes particular aim at Left-liberals working in a broadly Rawlsian tradition, critiquing them from a sophisticated Marxist position. One such Left-liberal is myself. Rossi references an older essay of mine for *Jacobin* as an example of positions becoming "somewhat popular of late" and so warranting rebuttal.[3]

But Rossi's main theoretical foil in his essay is not me, but John Rawls, the late American political philosopher best known for authoring *A Theory of Justice*. Rossi describes Rawls as "the foremost liberal theorist of the second half of the twentieth century," who exercises "unparalleled

---

1   Originally Printed in *Damage Magazine*. The following was written in response to an earlier critical article in *Damage* by Dr. Enzo Rossi.

2   Enzo Rossi, "Socialism Is Not Liberal Moralism on Steroids," *Damage*, February 2025.

3   Matt McManus, "The Left Should Reclaim John Rawls' Theory of Justice," *Jacobin*, September 2023.

influence within Anglophone academia." After a quick 101 on Rawlsian philosophy, Rossi admits that Rawls's theory of justice calls for a society "far more egalitarian than any society we've known" — even more so than social democracy. Given that private control of resources would be far more limited and wealth would be less concentrated if Rawls's theory were carried out, isn't this basically "just a few steps from socialism?"

Rossi says no for two reasons. I'll deal with the first here.

Rossi reads Rawls as being still committed to capitalism, and merely as tying it to the "ball and chain" of justice. In other words, Rawlsians want to maintain capitalist societies while insulating citizens from their worst consequences — for instance, by limiting inherited wealth. He admits that some Rawlsians have a "vision" that requires going further — for instance, limiting the capacity of capital to purchase labor. But by and large Rossi thinks most Left-liberals inevitably slip back into market reasoning; pondering how "it can be right to redistribute so much of the money they 'freely chose' to work for..." Such a failure of vision and nerve is at least one reason why Left-liberal social democratic projects ended up just being a "temporary concession" by capital.

The problem with this reading is that it doesn't really account for Rawls's own radicalness on any number of points. The first edition of *A Theory of Justice* notes that the question of whether a socialist system, a "private property system" or the "many intermediate forms most fully answer to the requirements of justice cannot, I think, be determined in advance." Whether one of these systems is to be chosen as the best to institute the principles of justice will depend "in large part upon the traditions, institutions, and social forces of each country, and its particular historical circumstances." Nothing at even this early point forecloses the possibility of socialism in Rawlsianism. And the choice for it must be made on materialist reasons of historical circumstance.

Contra Rossi, the late Rawls is unambiguously critical of "welfare state capitalism" (i.e., something very close to the social democratic states of the mid-twentieth century) for denying "fair value of the political liberties" through enabling the very wealthy to enjoy unequal power. Welfare-state capitalism also does not have sufficient concern for "equality of opportunity" and permits "very large inequalities in the ownership of real property... so that control of the economy and much of political life rests in a few hands." It does offer "quite generous" welfare provisions and a social minimum, but these do not rise to the level required by a "principle of reciprocity to regulate economic and social inequities..." Consequently Rawls concludes that only a "liberal socialist" or "property-owning democracy" (basically a society where private property would exist, but at a very small scale and more or less equally distributed) could satisfy his two principles of justice.

In his *Lectures on the History of Political Philosophy*, Rawls dedicates three talks to Marx, who is applauded for his "remarkable achievements", which count as "extraordinary, indeed heroic." Rawls reprimands those who think "Marx's socialist philosophy and economics are of no significance today" for making a "serious mistake." He goes on to outline four elements of the "illuminating and worthwhile view" of liberal socialism. A liberal socialist society requires 1) a constitutional democracy with robust political liberties; 2) a system of free competitive markets, ensured by law as necessary; 3) a scheme of worker-owned businesses managed by elected or firm-chosen managers; and 4) a property system establishing a more or less even distribution of the means of production and natural resources.

It's clear here that Rawlsian liberal socialism is committed to a view that goes explicitly beyond "welfare-state" social democracy. It is a kind of market socialism with guaranteed personal liberties and worker-owned firms to prevent concentrations of resources and power which could create inequalities in the value of citizens' "political liberties." This vision is explicitly indebted to Marxism and Marx, who is commended throughout Rawls' work. Rawls certainly had little time for the idea that it would be wrong to redistribute wealth someone has "worked" for.

Liberal Socialism and Ideology

Rossi's second and more powerful critique is that Left-liberals have largely been unable to theorize the nature of power under capitalism because of ideology. Liberals simply take desires, preferences and moral intuitions as given. That's the problem with their "justice talk": it's largely a discourse delimited by the dynamics of capitalism. It is constrained by the ideas and sentiments that are already prevalent within society as it is.

Consciousness is determined by economic life. Rossi's essentially epistemological claim is that liberal modes of cognition are so molded by capitalism that they simply cannot think their way past it in any meaningful sense. Inevitably they end up reproducing "status quo commitments" that befit the role of liberalism as the herald ideology of capitalism.

This view of liberals, especially liberal socialists, as simply taking desires, preferences and moral intuitions as a given is incorrect. From John Locke and Immanuel Kant's guides to educating free reasoners to Mary Wollstonecraft's fierce denunciation of how women and the poor were educated to induce their willing subordination, there has long been an abiding respect for critical thinking and pedagogy on the part of liberalism. John Stuart Mill, who himself identified as a liberal socialist, famously declared it was simply better to be an unhappy Socrates than a blue-pilled pig. Many others in the liberal socialist tradition would insist the same, following radicals like Chantal Mouffe in calling for a rejection of hegemony to adopt a more agonistic attitude toward power — especially the power of capital.

But Rossi is correct that one simply cannot compare the theoretical rigor and depth of Marxist and other critical traditions on ideology and hegemony to what one sees in the writing of Left-liberals today. Moreover, otherwise impressive liberal socialists from Mill to Rawls to Axel Honneth have by and large demonstrated a poor understanding of the nature of capitalism as a global system of mute compulsion. Some have followed Mill in defending imperialism for ideological or strategic reasons. Others were sympathetic to the need for worldwide changes à *la* Rawls but utterly failed to provide a compelling account of the current system of global political economy.

Nevertheless, many Left-liberals and liberal socialists have worked to sublate this limitation. Samuel Moyn has written about how even in the halcyon days of liberal internationalism, the commitment to rights for all the world was "not enough" to constitute a genuinely radical project.[4] Self-described black radical liberal Charles Mills, who endorsed a form of market socialism and Left economics near his death, drew heavily on Marxist theories of ideology to account for why right-wing liberals so readily endorsed imperialism and racist practices. Mills also chastised Rawls for being inadequately engaged in the material and historical realities and operating at the level of "ideal theory." In other words, Left-liberalism and liberal socialism are evolving and revitalized theoretical traditions addressing many of the criticisms Rossi has raised at a high level.

---

4   Samuel Moyn, *Not Enough*, Harvard, 2019.

Once More on Moral Philosophy

Rossi's most general critique isn't just directed against Left-liberalism/liberal socialism but moral philosophy and argumentation generally. Identifying with the "materialist Left" he associates with Marx, Rossi doesn't think we should be writing "recipe books for the cook shops of the future." Instead we should begin to cook and see how it turns out; achieving socialism through a unity of theory that aims to describe the world and praxis that aspires to change it. It's worth quoting Rossi here in full:

> If there's a single ideal that guides the materialist Left, it isn't a moral ideal. It is an aspiration to strengthen our grasp of how the world works and how present dynamics limit our imaginations, to improve the position from which we make political choices. This is the sense in which our conception of emancipation is different from the liberal one: rather than striving for the freedom to get whatever we want here and now, we try to create conditions under which our desires are truly our own. That requires radically dispersing power as widely as possible, away from the elite of owners and bosses, and in ways that don't let the profit motive become a primary drive. The aim is to genuinely leave people to their own devices, in the hope — and this really is little more than an educated hope — that they will be able to figure out a better way to live together, as individuals. The freedom to try to fulfill one's individual preferences while at the mercy of market forces will be transformed into the freedom to collectively self-determine our priorities, to create space for genuine individual flourishing.

I have nothing against using theory to describe the world. Nor, to be clear, do any Left-liberals or liberal socialists. But there is something extremely odd in claiming to eschew moral theory and argumentation before appealing to "our conception of emancipation," the creation of "conditions under which our desires are truly our own," and the "freedom to collectively self-determine our priorities" in order to establish spaces of "genuine individual flourishing." These are paradigmatically moral ideals — indeed, both socialist and *liberal* ideals. Rossi may argue that he is not interested in theoretically defending these socialist ideals, but rather only in using theory to anticipate the conditions under which the ideals might be realized in practice. That's a swell project, but it also means that the ethical ideals of socialism are either implicitly assumed to be correct, or at best that there is nothing valuable to be gained by explicating the ethical ideals and arguing for them clearly.

In either case I think it is a mistake. There can be nothing gained by constraining or chiding socialist thinkers for offering arguments for moral ideals we have good reasons to endorse. The correct attitude would seem to be: from each socialist thinker according to his ability, to each according to the rigor and impact of their case.

Liberal socialist thinkers have good reason to dedicate more time to describing the real world of power, and for focusing less on ideal theoretical moral arguments. But the inverse is true of any Marxists and materialists who until the late twentieth century often got by on the now completely discredited idea that science simply showed that socialism was the future — whether one thought it a good future or not. We don't need to write recipe books, but it's useful to think about what kind of dish we ought to make with the ingredients on hand.

This brings me back round to liberal socialism. Whatever Rossi thinks, it is not simply a "self-description." It is simply a historical fact that thinkers from John Stuart Mill to Norberto Bobbio to Chantal Mouffe and Carlo Rosselli identified as liberal socialists and thought it a regime worth defending. I attempt to retrieve the political theory of liberal socialism by arguing it is defined by three core principles: methodological collectivism and normative individualism, a developmental rather than acquisitive ethic, and a commitment to achieving the democratization of the economy and family within a liberal constitutional framework guaranteeing equal basic rights — but excluding rights to private ownership of the means of production. These principles have often been inadequately defended by many liberal socialists, who to my mind were never Marxist enough. But they remain attractive moral ideals worthy of loyalty.

LIBERALISM AFTER TRUMP[1]

Liberalism has been in crisis for the better part of a decade now. The meanings of the 2024 election will be hotly debated, but one thing isn't up for discussion: It proved that Trumpism isn't some freakish aberration from hegemonic American liberalism, a kind of once-and-done roll of the dice on the part of the people. It has gained real traction, in no small part because a decisive number of voters no longer want to buy what American liberals are selling.

This is a major comedown from the "Hope and Change" aspirations of the Obama years, when many thought the 2008 GOP defeat signaled a sea change in the electorate. Unfortunately, many liberals don't appear interested in learning from the global surge of Right populism and anti-elitism. Indeed, plenty seem happy to insist that the problem wasn't American liberalism but the American people not being good enough to live up to liberal expectations. Until we liberals recognize why we keep failing, we will never stop. Understanding liberalism's history will clarify the reasons for our present failures.

Liberalism is not one thing but a family of doctrines. All forms of liberalism share certain core principles and attitudes. But just as someone might be a member of your family and still lead you to wonder how you're related, liberals often disagree vehemently with one another about

---

1   Originally printed in *Compact Magazine*.

the right way to interpret and apply the doctrine. But one kind of liberalism beat out the others, and we are suffering the consequences of its ascent and failures.

As Samuel Moyn writes in his book *Liberalism Against Itself*, liberalism first emerged as a fighting creed. Liberals believed that the *ancien regime* was sclerotic, superstitious, ill-organized and domineering. The old feudal system was predicated on a vision of society that Charles Taylor describes as hierarchical complementarity,[2] in which status is inherited and fixed. Against this, liberals developed a theory of egalitarianism drawing on older Christian and Stoic themes — all men are moral equals and entitled to govern themselves. Liberal egalitarianism provided the intellectual underpinnings for the American, French and Haitian revolutions. Although there is a history of liberals acting hypocritically — like the Founding Father's toleration of slavery — many forms of liberalism remained visionary, progressive and optimistic. Arch liberal J.S. Mill even called himself a socialist and argued for wealth redistribution and the democratization of firms. The American liberal John Rawls was also very friendly to socialist reforms to democratize the economy and do justice by the least well-off.[3]

Moyn points out this began to change in the middle of the twentieth century when a much more conservative and elitist form of "Cold War liberalism" became intellectually and eventually politically ascendant. Cold War liberals worried that the more visionary, progressive kinds of liberalism were potential stepping stones to totalitarian serfdom. They were particularly worried about excesses of economic

---

2   Charles Taylor, *Modern Social Imaginaries*, Duke, 2003.
3   William A. Edmundsom, *John Rawls: Reticent Socialis*, Cambridge, 2017.

egalitarianism and democracy. Cold War liberals marginalized and banished their more progressive peers and worked to realign major Western parties around their vision of a cautious, elitist, very capitalist-friendly kind of liberalism.

This was a major mistake for many reasons, but I'll single out one. As Ronald Beiner notes in his magisterial *Civil Religion*, the right-wing critique liberalism has always been most vulnerable to is that it is a philosophy that brings about mediocrity and narrow horizons. As Nietzsche would put it, liberalism is an outlook fit for shopkeeping last men. Beiner points out that this neglects the often heroic history of liberalism's revolutions against the aristocracy, which even Marx applauded. But by defensively turning to Cold War liberalism, or what Alexandre Lefebvre (invoking Kierkegaard) calls a kind of faux liberaldom,[4] liberals became very vulnerable to accusations of being stultifying, moralistic technocrats and elitists. In hindsight it's clear the most dangerous path liberals could take was the one taken: to narrow liberalism's aspirations along the lines demanded by Cold War liberals and moderate conservatives. To become a liberalism of fear rather than hope.

The results have been disastrous, above all for liberals. In *National Populism: The Revolt Against Liberal Democracy*, social scientists Roger Eatwell and Matthew Goodwin show how voters in many countries perceive liberal elites to be out of touch, unresponsive to voters and prone to implementing policies that help other elites and not ordinary people. These perceptions are grounded in reality. Regardless of which party comes to power, a plutocracy reigns. This was spectacularly evident in the 2024 election, when Democrats enjoyed more big donations than their GOP rivals, but Trump was supported by mega-billionaires

---

4 Alexandre Lefebvre, *Liberalism as a Way of Life*, Princeton, 2024.

like Elon Musk and others and now looks set to enjoy wide oligarchic support.

Polls show that the public supports the rich paying more,[5] raising the minimum wage,[6] and Medicare for all,[7] and yet American liberals have done notably little to advance those goals. Or worse, they make promises they do not keep. These failures reflect the antiquated shibboleths of Cold War liberalism: that big swings are to be avoided, expertise must go unquestioned even when shown to be wrong, and establishment centrists are to be preferred to their more radical challengers.

Despite these failings, I do not think that liberalism has truly "failed." A majority of Americans support gay marriage, abortion in some circumstances, and decriminalization of drugs.[8] Despite his anti-elitist populism, Trump has surrounded himself with his own set of plutocrats. Liberals have the opportunity to rejuvenate the more visionary, egalitarian and hopeful facets of their doctrine by offering an agenda that actually challenges elites and

---

5   *Polling Matters*, "Average American Remains OK with Higher Taxes on Rich," August 2022: https://news.gallup.com/opinion/polling-matters/396737/average-american-remains-higher-taxes-rich.aspx

6   Amina Dunn, "Most Americans Support a 15$ Minimum Wage," *Pew Research Center*, April 2021: https://www.pewresearch.org/short-reads/2021/04/22/most-americans-support-a-15-federal-minimum-wage/

7   Julia Conley, "62% of Americans Agree US Government Should Ensure Everyone Has Health Coverage," *Common Dreams*, December 2024: https://www.commondreams.org/news/universal-healthcare-poll

8   *Pew Research Center*, "Most Americans Favor Legalizing Marijuana for Medical, Recreational Use," March 2024: https://www.pewresearch.org/politics/2024/03/26/most-americans-favor-legalizing-marijuana-for-medical-recreational-use/

makes life better for ordinary people. I've proposed a kind of liberal socialism;[9] other proposals should come to the fore.

Some of the more reflective post-election commentary by liberals acknowledged it was a mistake to run machine politicians against an angry populist like Trump who can tap into anti-system animus. That is very much the case. Liberals have spent too much time approaching politics like a numbers game, where a winning coalition can be cobbled together by giving each well-defined demographic a (minimal) bundle of goods and attention. Far too little attention has been paid to presenting a unifying vision. Aligned with this, liberals must recover the Rooseveltian courage to denounce plutocracy in direct and personal terms. And above all else, liberals need to remember that securing liberty and equality for all doesn't just mean establishing a rainbow-colored ruling class. It means ensuring liberty, equality and fraternity are real for everyone.

---

9   Matt McManus, *The Political Theory of Liberal Socialism*, Routledge 2025.

FROM THE ABSTRACT TO THE CONCRETE: THE SELF-REFLEXIVITY OF THE LIBERAL SUBJECT

By Florian Maiwald

One of the fundamental questions in the development of political theory — and thus also of political philosophy — consists (even if this may at first seem like an inadmissible reduction of complexity) in finding an answer to how human beings should deal with the inescapable fact of their freedom. In short: how people can be enabled to cope with the circumstance that, by their very nature, they must be regarded as liberal subjects. This form of freedom manifests itself not only in concrete questions of political theory but also in everyday phenomena. For example, when we as individuals concern ourselves with planning our day or even our lives: Which profession should I choose (provided I have the options)? Should I tell her that I love her, or, even further along, should I propose to her? How should I balance discipline and hedonism in my life? Do I prefer to get up early or sleep long?

Should I have another drink, or go home early to avoid the agonies of a hangover?

The postulation of the liberal subject is a necessary anthropological assumption for any form of political theory (including, or especially, the liberal socialist approach). Nevertheless, it is legitimate in this context to ask what exactly is meant with liberal forms of subjectivity.

Erich Fromm, in his essay on disobedience in which he discusses the expulsion of Adam and Eve from Paradise[1], was able to express with great clarity what might be described as the liberal subject. In short: that liberalism — and the freedom associated with it — must be regarded as an inescapable aspect of the human condition. Or, as Alexander Lefebvre puts it in his book *Liberalism as a Way of Life*: liberalism as a worldview is like the water in which we swim. Thus, liberalism is not merely a specific way of organizing institutional, economic and social conditions, but also a particular form of subjective disposition, and therefore shapes the way in which people relate to themselves and to their environment.[2]

If one reads Fromm closely, one can see — albeit within a theological framework (though he also illustrates this idea beyond theological contexts) — that liberal forms of subjectivity are characterized by two essential traits: 1) the fact of *inevitability* — that is, people have no option but to understand themselves as inherently liberal subjects. And 2): the liberal subject is marked by an inherent form of *self-reflexivity*. According to Fromm, the inevitability of liberalism — or, in Lefebvre's terms, the reason why

---

1   Cf. Erich Fromm, *Über den Ungehorsam und andere Essays* 1981, 5. Translated from German to English.

2   Cf. Alexandre Lefebvre, *Liberalism as a Way of Life*, Princeton, 2024, 11–12.

liberalism (specifically, freedom) is to be regarded as the water in which we swim — can be explained by the fact of becoming human, and thus the capacity to understand oneself as a subject, cannot be explained without a constitutive act of disobedience. In Fromm's reading, resistance to God's command not to eat from the tree of knowledge not only leads to Adam and Eve's expulsion from Paradise, but this expulsion — and thus the initial destruction of the harmonious state in the Garden of Eden — is characterized by an unavoidable inescapability. Fromm's thesis is that the process of humanization (and the principle of free action inextricably linked to it) can only be understood through this original act of disobedience, by which Adam and Eve were able to defy the divine command.

If one reads Fromm closely, the act of disobedience performed by Adam and Eve is not only characterized by inevitability (expulsion and becoming human) but also elucidates a central characteristic of liberal forms of subjectivity: the capacity for self-reflexivity. In this context, self-reflexivity should not merely describe specific forms of psychological introspection, but rather the fact that human beings (as subjects) establish a reflexive relationship between themselves and the social circumstances surrounding them. To remain within Fromm's theologically embedded argumentative framework: the process of self-reflexivity is associated with a rebellion against a specifically prevailing form of power structure. To put it more concretely: human freedom — which, it should be noted, Fromm understands as a phenomenon marked by ambivalence — is inconceivable without the subversion of specific forms of domination (here symbolized by divine authority).[3]

---

3   Cf. ibid.

From Fromm's example, one can not only illustrate how the fact of self-reflexivity is to be regarded as an anthropological constant, but also why this anthropological constant can serve as a central normative foundation for liberal socialist forms of theory-building. Whether one begins with the revolt of the bourgeoisie against feudal and absolutist structures or with the uprising of the industrial proletariat against capitalist modes of economic organization, in all these processes of subversion exercised by human beings it becomes clearly evident that an originally (seemingly) harmonious telos — in this context: the feudal social structures or the Garden of Eden — has the capacity to provoke a form of discomfort within the human subject and is consequently subjected to concrete processes of change. While the bourgeois revolt against feudal structures was an important and necessary step toward a higher degree of freedom, the later emergence of the proletarian subject reveals that these subversive processes must be understood as an unfinished project. This becomes most apparent when Marx, in the *Eighteenth Brumaire*, points out that the abstract freedoms the bourgeoisie managed to wrest from the feudal regime were ultimately, with the rise of the proletarian subject, turned against the bourgeoisie itself.

Marx states:

> The bourgeoisie had the correct insight that all the weapons it forged against feudalism turned their points against itself; that all the means of education it created rebelled against its own civilization; that all the gods it had fashioned had deserted it. It understood that all the so-called bourgeois freedoms and organs of progress simultaneously attacked and threatened its class rule both at the social base and at

the political apex — that is, they had become "socialist."[4]

The conflict-ridden potential of liberal forms of subjectivity — in short: the sense that they are in constant antagonism to the existing order — becomes clearly apparent in the unease of the proletarian subject. The proletarian subject shares with the bourgeois subject the rebellion against any form of power structure that contributes to a restriction of their own freedom and the subsequent process of critically and self-reflexively relating to the prevailing circumstances. The concrete difference between the proletarian and bourgeois constitution of subjectivity, however, can be located in the understanding of what is to be regarded as a freedom-restricting factor. More specifically: the transition from the bourgeois to the proletarian subject expresses the transition from the abstract to the concrete, and thus the transition from a purely liberal to a democratic-socialist conception of freedom. As Ed Rooksby aptly elaborated, it is precisely the universalism of freedom and equality implicit in bourgeois ideals that ensures that these initially abstract ideals become concrete in the course of the workers' struggle, as large sections of the population become increasingly aware of the blatant discrepancy between these bourgeois ideals and the devastating economic conditions they are confronted with.[5] Thus, the liberal subject, in the original sense, is to be regarded as the bearer of the socialist progression, in which the transition from the abstract to the concrete takes place. None other than Carlo Rosselli himself

---

4   Karl Marx, *The 18th Brumaire of Louis Bonaparte.* Translated from German.
5   Cf. Ed Rooksby, "The Relationship Between Liberalism and Socialism," *Science and Society*, 76(4), 2012, 508: https://www.jstor.org/stable/41714354?seq=1

pointed out how this form of transition comes to bear within the liberal socialist approach itself:

> Socialism is nothing more than the logical development, taken to its extreme consequences, of the principle of liberty. Socialism, when understood in its fundamental sense and judged by its results — as the concrete movement for the emancipation of the proletariat — is liberalism in action; it means that liberty comes into the life of poor people. Socialism says: the abstract recognition of liberty of conscience and political freedoms for all, though it may represent an essential moment in the development of political theory, is a thing of very limited value when the majority of men, forced to live as a result of circumstances of birth and environment in moral and material poverty, are left without the possibility of appreciating its significance and taking any actual advantage of it.[6]

Here too, Rosselli clearly emphasizes how, within the liberal socialist framework, the transition from abstract conceptions of freedom translates into the concrete, material conditions of human beings. Or, as Matthew McManus aptly expresses in his seminal work on the liberal socialist theoretical approach, the concept of freedom within liberal socialist theory is grounded in a *methodologically collectivist social ontology* combined with a *normative individualism*. In essence, freedom and individuality should be the ultimate aim of any political endeavor. However, the means to achieve this goal must acknowledge that human beings — even as

---

6   Carlo Rosselli and Nadia Urbinati, ed. *Liberal Socialism*, 2017, 86.

liberal subjects — are fundamentally interdependent creatures.[7]

In other words: only in this way does the truly liberal subject come to find itself and finally becomes able to fulfill the promise of freedom.[8]

---

7   Cf. Matt McManus, *The Political Theory of Liberal Socialism*, Routledge, 2025, 18.

8   In my book *Ein sozialistischer Liberaler oder ein liberaler Sozialist? (A Socialist Liberal or a Liberal Socialist?)* — which is up until now available only in German — I aim to demonstrate that the anthropological assumptions underlying J.S. Mill's political theory lead to a perspective that transcends the traditional foundations of both liberalism and socialism. In brief, these anthropological foundations — especially evident in Mill's *Logic* — form the basis for a theoretical approach that can be described as liberal socialist.

AGAINST THE FREEDOM OF THE CHAINSAW, OR: WHY ONLY A LIBERAL SOCIALISM CAN SAVE US

By Florian Maiwald

Symbols can indeed be powerful tools for intellectually grasping the prevailing spirit of the times. If one is searching for a symbol that aptly captures our current era, the chainsaw seems particularly appropriate — for it illustrates how the very principle of freedom, through its own radicalization, is carried to the point of absurdity. At first, it matters little whether one is referring to tech-libertarianism or some form of anarcho-capitalism. The image was first employed by Javier Milei to promote the destruction of the Argentine state apparatus, and later by Elon Musk, who systematically sought to dismantle American bureaucracy with DOGE.[1] However, it can hardly be the aim here

---

1   Cf. Evans S., "Milei Offers a Chainsaw to Musk: The Bureaucracy Better Watch Out!" *Cointribune*, February 2025: https://www.cointribune.com/en/milei-offers-a-chainsaw-to-musk-the-bureaucracy-better-watch-out/

to offer a comprehensive analysis of the prevailing political landscape.

Far more intriguing, however, is the question of what the symbol of the chainsaw implies for the very concept of freedom itself. Put succinctly, and to borrow from Adorno, one might contend that, in this context, we are confronted with an abstract form of negation that finds its expression symbolically. In other words: the essence of the chainsaw resides in pure negation — specifically, in the destruction of existing institutional, economic and social structures — rather than in the affirmative endorsement of any alternative model of society.[2]

Particularly fascinating in this context is the name of Milei's party: *La Libertad Avanza* (in English: "Freedom Advances"). The paradox of this motto, however, lies precisely in the fact that a libertarian-authoritarian conception of freedom — to draw on the theoretical framework elaborated by Carolin Amlinger and Oliver Nachtwey[3] — transcends a purely negative notion of liberty (one in which the individual is free from all external constraints) through an abstract negation of everything that exists.

Rather, such a concept of freedom, true to the name of Milei's party, pushes toward the total negation, and thus the very impossibility, of negative forms of freedom themselves. In short: even the ability to conceive of oneself as an atomized subject, or, in Marx's terms, as an isolated monad (an early stage of liberal subjectivity),[4]

---

2   Cf. Theodor Adorno, *Negative Dialektik*, Suhrkamp, 1966, 124. Translated from German.

3   Cf. Caroline Amlinger and Oliver Nachtwey, *Gekränkte Freiheit*, Suhrkamp, 2022.

4   Karl Marx, *Zur Judenfrage*, 1844, 15: https://is.cuni.cz/studium/predmety/index.php?do=download&did=151721&kod-

presupposes specific conditions (namely, the existence of other atomized subjects) from which the individual can distinguish itself.

Liberal forms of subjectivity rest upon a distinct anthropological assumption — one that is equally significant for the liberal socialist perspective: namely, that human beings desire to act as active agents in shaping their own lives and, by extension, the circumstances that surround them. This understanding of the human condition has far-reaching implications for the very concept of freedom: the realization of freedom itself depends upon particular forms of economic and social organization. Put even more succinctly: the negation of those concrete conditions within which individuals are first able to realize their freedom ultimately results in the negation of the very idea of freedom itself.

It is only through the limitation of one's own freedom that the possibility arises for freedom to be fully realized. (Rhough we must be caution here against assuming that there exists some inner human essence that merely needs to be "unfolded" — even from a Left-progressive perspective, Isaiah Berlin has raised a significant objection in this regard that should not be underestimated.[5])

Authors such as Axel Honneth have subsumed this approach under the concept of "social freedom,"[6] while in Marx it finds paradigmatic expression in the assertion that the "the free development of each is the condition for the

---

=ADE100174 (Translated from German).

5   Cf. Isaiah Berlin, *Zwei Freiheitsbegriffe*, De Gruyter, 1958, 153.

6   Cf. Rutger Claassen, "Social Freedom and the Demands of Justice: A Study of Honneth's *Recht Der Freiheit*," *Constellations*, 21(1), 2014, 69–70.

free development of all".[7] Nevertheless, it would be mistaken to believe that there will ever be a perfectly harmonious state in which individuals can fully realize their potential.

Balibar's concept of *equaliberty* vividly demonstrates that the liberal subject is characterized by an inescapable inner tension — a tension that must, in turn, be understood as a necessary precondition for liberal forms of subjectivity and, furthermore, as an appropriate anthropological foundation for the liberal socialist approach.

Elsewhere, I have argued that self-reflexivity — that is, the capacity of the subject to conceive of itself in fundamental antagonism to the existing order — is a central characteristic of liberal subjectivity. This self-reflexivity, in turn, cannot be understood without reference to that very form of inner tension which has shaped liberal anthropology from the outset. When Balibar states that "the negation of freedom in fact destroys equality, and the negation of equality in fact destroys freedom,"[8] he captures the torn nature of the liberal subject with great precision.

What is most interesting in this context, however, is that the principle of *equaliberty* is marked by a kind of perpetual incompleteness. Put differently — and applied to the present context — the liberal subject exists in a constant tension between individuality and community: equality without freedom can give rise to new forms of domination, while freedom without egalitarian structures remains abstract and may result in powerlessness.

In this context, Irving Howe not only pointed to the emancipatory potential of the liberal subject — which,

---

7   Karl Marx and Friedrich Engels, *Manifesto of the Communist Party*, 1848, 27: https://www.marxists.org/archive/marx/works/download/pdf/Manifesto.pdf

8   Balibar, 2012, 174 (Translated from German to English).

according to Howe, socialists often fail to recognize — but also to the fact that while freedom may indeed depend on egalitarian structures in order to be meaningfully realized, the most fundamental basis for legitimizing the creation of such egalitarian structures should, in turn, be the freedom of the individual itself:

> Still, who does not feel the continued poignancy in the yearning for community, which seems so widespread in our time? Who does not respond, in our society, to the cry that life is poor in shared experiences, vital communities, free brother (sister) hoods? Yet precisely the pertinence and power of this attack upon traditional liberalism must leave one somewhat uneasy. For we must remember that we continue to live in a time when the yearning for community has been misshaped into a gross denial of personal integrity, when the desire for the warmth of social bonds — marching together, living together, huddling together, complaining in concert — has helped to betray a portion of the world into the shame of the total state.[9]

As the arguments of Balibar and Howe make clear, socialism can ultimately only take the form of a liberal socialism. In this context, it is important to emphasize that the liberal socialist theoretical approach must, for precisely this reason, be understood as an open-ended project: its aim is not to achieve a fully harmonious social telos in which everyone — as Marx once envisioned — can develop their capacities entirely free from conflict. Rather, the liberal socialist approach fully recognizes that the tension between individual

---

9   Irving Howe, "Socialism and Liberalism: Articles of Control," *Dissent*, Winter 1977, 29: https://www.dissentmagazine.org/wp-content/files_mf/1433357734winter77howe.pdf

and community can never be entirely resolved. Freedom, instead, is conceived as a never-ending struggle for emancipation — both the emancipation of the individual from the oppressive tendencies of the egalitarian community, and, at the same time, the emancipation of equality from the brutality that the primacy of freedom can entail: namely (to return to the earlier point) the abstract negation of those structural conditions whose egalitarian foundation makes individual freedom possible in the first place.

INHERITANCE OF EQUALS: A CASE FOR LIBERAL SOCIALISM

by Paul Crider

In place of the old bourgeois society, with its classes and class antagonisms, we shall have an association, in which the free development of each is the condition for the free development of all.
  Karl Marx and Friedrich Engels, *The Communist Manifesto*,
1848

...make it a government of the people, by the people and for the people, and for all the people, each for all and all for each.
  Frederick Douglass, "Sources of Danger to the Republic,"
1867

That each individual is afforded a fair opportunity to develop their personality and individual faculties freely. That society comprises free and equal beings, where freedom means freedom from undue interference, freedom from domination and oppression, freedom of collective action and self-governance, and freedom to develop and expand human capabilities. That neither one's family and place of birth determine one's destiny, nor bad luck nor the normal human range of vice and folly. That no person or cabal has overwhelming, unchecked power by means of wealth or influence, no matter how attained. These are the sentiments undergirding liberal socialism.

The cruel lawlessness of the Trump-Musk regime will eventually pass. With it, the institutional liquefaction will cease, and some new constitutional configuration will settle into place. Things literally cannot go on as they have before the present democratic crisis—things have been broken and will have to be put back together somehow. There is opportunity in this. Ideas that were unthinkable even a decade ago may see their chance in the sun.

It is time for liberal socialism.

Democratic when the world's democracies are on the defensive, resolutely liberal when politicians and electorates are eager to throw vulnerable groups like immigrants and trans men and women to the wolves, and suspicious of concentrated wealth when the fascist vanguard is led by billionaire oligarchs—liberal socialism is the antithesis of MAGA. As a political faction, liberal socialists are a bulwark against fascism, and constitute the natural anchor of a popular front antifascist coalition, smoothing antagonisms between mutually suspicious leftists and liberals. My purpose with this essay is to make liberals and socialists intelligible to one another. A vocal adoption of the liberal socialist moniker itself connects ideas and partisans long thought unbridgeable.

But isn't liberal socialism an oxymoron?

Perhaps I'm getting ahead of myself. No, liberal socialism is not an oxymoron. Though distinct traditions, liberalism and socialism are both broad and varied, with significant overlap. Liberal socialism sounds untenable, if not contradictory, due to our collective hangover from the Cold War. For most of the twentieth century, the dominant strain of socialism was that of the USSR, the global superpower that represented a genuine threat to the US and the liberal democratic world broadly.

Soviet socialism wasn't the fun kind. It involved one-party dictatorship, violent domestic repression and imperialism abroad, and forced collectivization of agriculture that led to deadly famines. The central planning at the core of Stalinism led to rolling economic catastrophes across decades. Liberals really did have the socialists' number in the theoretical "socialist calculation debate," but the proof was in the empirical pudding. The later, even deadlier example of Maoist communism only hardened liberals against socialism. These horrors didn't stop socialists in the First World from taking their ideological cues from the Soviets and the CCP.

Who could blame the classical and conservative liberals of the twentieth century for thinking of socialism as inherently antiliberal given these examples? But with the fall of the Iron Curtain, socialists have largely moved away from central planning and violent revolution and toward democratic values. Now, the greatest enemy of liberal democracy is the oligarch-sponsored reactionary right, an enemy shared by socialists. There is every reason for the liberal and the socialist to reappraise their relationship.

Do you even read theory?

Liberalism defines itself in terms of freedom, and liberal socialism is no different. But the freedom of liberal socialism is ambitious and expansive, mingling and interpenetrating with equality like a yin and yang. We will see that equality is necessary for and constitutive of freedom, and vice versa.

But first, the libertarians are right: freedom from interference is a genuine kind of freedom. There is such a thing as going about one's own business, and interfering with that business requires compelling reason. Republicans (that's a small-r) have long described freedom as freedom from domination. No person should be subject to the arbitrary will of another, whether that external will has good or ill intentions. These kinds of freedom can conflict. The struggle for freedom from domination has been interpreted in various times and places as interfering with the property rights of the slave owner, or the private domain of the husband.

Oppression is disadvantage experienced by individuals owing to their perceived group memberships, and arises from systematic patterns of privilege and prejudice. If the free development of each is to be the condition for the free development of all, then freedom from oppression is crucial. Oppression is distinct from domination because domination can be purely personal. Freedom from oppression is often set in opposition to freedom from interference because oppression can be achieved by the unknowing and unwilling actions of people going about their business. Liberation from oppression requires interference.

It's helpful to think of freedom as the ability to make our agency impact reality. But we have designs on the world we can't realize by individual action alone. They must be achieved by collective action or not at all. Thus, freedom to act in coordination with others is necessary. This is democracy expressed in terms of freedom. Collective decision-making is an obvious vector of interference of the individual and of oppression. This kind of freedom is the hardest to harmonise with naïve liberalism as it leads us to a politics of inevitable conflict.

In the above I've borrowed heavily from the liberal theorist Sharon Krause. But I'll add one more freedom that Krause elides: freedom as capability. New abilities to be and act in the world are real extensions of freedom. The airplane opened the wide world to us. With the Internet, we could communicate and commune with others in a way that was impossible before. With the birth control pill, women were liberated from their wombs in a practical way that feminist awakening alone could never achieve. Modern hormone therapy and gender-affirming care allow countless individuals—cis and trans alike—to be their true selves in a way they recognize. This is, perhaps, the most abstract kind of freedom theoretically while being simple to understand in practical life: the washing machine is freedom. Yet new technologies, both social and material, also offer new possibilities for interference, domination, oppression, and coordination.

Liquidating the plutocrats...as a class.

Liberals can often be relied on to defend civic equality—equal political rights and formal equality before the law. Liberals also at least pay lip service to social equality, the idea that one's various identities and social groups should not bear an overly deterministic relationship to one's life outcomes. In practice, of course, conservative and moderate liberals often buy into narratives that demonise, denigrate, or blame various groups. The conservative work ethic that blames the poor for not working hard enough while assuming the rich deserve their wealth is a good example of this.

By contrast, traditional liberals, with some exceptions, have often failed to see economic equality as a genuine value that is distinct from economic sufficiency and protection from elite predation. If everyone has enough (by some standard), and the wealth of the rich was acquired without violence or fraud, then that wealth must be legitimate. Besides, economic equality is inherently unstable. The moment individuals begin trading or even just using their resources for different purposes, inequality emerges.

A key pillar of liberal socialism is that stark inequality itself is an evil that demands rectification and guarding against. I say stark inequality because, of course, some differences in wealth and income are inevitable and benign. But logarithmic differences in wealth, where lone persons command wealth comparable to the incomes of whole nations, signal disordered political economies and represent intrinsic threats to political order.

Libertarians sometimes argue that inequality of this magnitude cannot arise but by corruption and crony capitalism, and so these problems should be addressed directly rather than attacking the symptom—wealth inequality. There's some truth to this, but it shifts the burden of justification from the plutocrat to the egalitarian reformer who must show in detail how an individual's wealth accreted unjustly. Meanwhile the plutocrats use their vast resources to dazzle and confuse a public already predisposed by human nature to fawn over the rich and powerful.

In reality, any extreme concentration of wealth both hails from injustice in the past and portends injustice in the future. It's a brute fact of history that if you go back far enough (you usually don't have to go back very far) you will find conquest, exploitation, and rapine. The "original positions" of all social contract theories just abstract away from this reality of unequal regimes. But this fact alone gives no direction for the future. We can't go back. We don't want to.

But even if massive wealth somehow managed to concentrate itself into the hands of a few lucky or exceptional individuals by innocent means, injustice would inevitably follow. It's a time-tested proverb that power corrupts, and vast wealth surrounded by lesser means is a kind of power. Its very presence in one set of hands constitutes domination—the rest of us rightly tremble that on a moment's fancy the billionaire will turn his awesome materials on some office or tribe that offends him.

Philosophical and religious traditions across the globe and spanning millennia have all warned against economic inequality, from the ancient Hebrews, Christians, and Platonists, to Thomas Hobbes, Adam Smith, and Karl Marx. These traditions talk about the psychological risks of extreme wealth. It becomes addicting, an obsession whereby no amount of wealth is ever enough. The truth of this is evident in the uniform tendency for the ultrarich to squirrel away their wealth in tax havens and exploit every possible loophole in the tax laws. Those who have literally more wealth than they could consume in several lifetimes can have no purpose other than the pleonectic quest for more and status competition with other billionaires.

Billionaires live in warped social environments where they're unable to have authentic human relationships. They don't have to interact with normal people in their everyday lives. Everyone they interact with only does so because of their massive wealth, either because they have been directly hired by the billionaire or because they are a representative of some organization or government asking for money. Everyone is sucking up. Even if one of a billionaire's legion of hirelings wanted to be honest, the risk is too great to say anything the billionaire might not want to hear—everyone is expendable and can be replaced. It's too easy, too tempting, to surround oneself with sycophants.

Think of concentrated wealth as just another dangerous thing that calls for social precaution and control. Liberal democracies regulate the use and ownership of firearms because they're inherently dangerous. Many weapons and firearms we ban outright. A billionaire is like an individual owning a massive arsenal of modern military weaponry, from machine guns and bazookas to tanks and submarines—even nukes—all with absolute impunity. At any moment, these private armies could cause untold carnage. Even if these weapons are never used, their mere presence in the hands of someone unaccountable to the public is a threat. The rest of us have to walk on eggshells.

It's no exaggeration to compare hectobillionaire wealth to this kind of private military. The proof surrounds us. Elon Musk has used his billions to turn a valuable public forum into a Nazi propaganda outlet. He has used his Starlink satellites to influence global geopolitics. He interfered in the 2024 US election by bribing voters and violating campaign finance laws, and tried to influence the 2025 German elections. Legal accountability is virtually impossible because he can exhaust all adversaries with lawsuits, countersuits, and endless appeals, making a sham of legal equality. And he's used his influence with President Trump to gain an unconfirmed, illegal position of undefined authority in the government. When you are wealthy enough, you are as a nation unto yourself.

The liberal socialist understands economic equality broadly as wealth ranging from no less than enough to thrive as a respectable member of one's community to strictly less than what one could use to dominate and destabilise the political order. Economic equality within this range is less a constraint on economic liberty and more the precondition for the wide-ranging freedom liberal socialists value. In order to secure freedom from domination, tax and fiscal policies should directly aim to erode high concentrations of economic power, including by progressive wealth and inheritance taxes. We can limit the kinds of industries that wealthy persons can own simultaneously to prevent oligarchic control of media and defense conglomerates. And wealthy individuals who are presently using their immense resources to attack democracies should simply have their wealth nationalised.

A better way is possible.

Wealth inequality is just one gross power differential. We can generalise to other kinds of power that fuel domination and oppression. Liberal socialists focus on empowering labor relative to capital, workers against owners and bosses, both within firms and across economic sectors.

Workplaces can be sites of tyranny where workers have virtually no control over their environments or the direction of their work. Bosses can be petty, domineering, and cruel. Workers have little recourse because of the steep cost of quitting—potential poverty and loss of healthcare for example—and the uncertainty of finding better alternatives. Bosses can even interfere with workers' private lives outside of work, retaliating against political activism and social media activities. As Elizabeth Anderson notes in *Private Government*, bosses and capitalists act toward workers in ways that we would describe as dictatorial in a political context, yet we spend about a quarter of our lives at work. That's a quarter of a person's life where they're expected to take tyranny on the chin.

Rectifying the power imbalances that make such tyranny possible requires reforms both inside and outside the workplace. Labor unions should be easy to organise, encouraged by policy, and protected by law. We can require firms of a certain size to include labor representation elected by workers on the board of directors. Sectoral bargaining can protect similar workers across an economy, decreasing inequality and narrowing gender and racial wage gaps. And workplace regulation should ensure people can go to work without fearing for their life and limb.

Whether firms succeed through peerless innovation or through crony capitalism, concentrated power in the market is just as dangerous as concentrated power in government or civil society. We can use anti-monopoly policies against market dominance that inhibits competition. The purpose here isn't to punish or champion any firm, but to establish a market that efficiently serves the public.

It's important to build up the economic power of the least advantaged apart from and prior to the wage relation. Experiments consistently reveal that a basic income of some kind—UBI, negative income tax, etc.—improves recipients' lives without perverse behavioral effects. A guaranteed income gives you a way out of oppressive situations, whether a bad boss, an unsafe job, or an abusive home life. No one should be forced to take on dangerous or demeaning work in order to keep a roof over their head or food on their kids' plates.

While a basic income can help sustain you, it can't supply the kind of peace of mind a flush bank account or a prosperous family can. It also does little to address wealth inequality, which depends on the actual assets households own. Such assets—land, homes, businesses, stock portfolios, etc.—pass from one generation to the next, piling wealth on wealth. The black-white racial wealth gap in particular has doggedly persisted over decades because of the systematic historical exclusion of blacks from asset bonanzas (like the Homestead Act), exclusion (red-lining), or basic violence and expropriation (like the Tulsa massacre). We can address this directly by a citizen's stakeholder grant of some amount large enough to buy a modest home or a college education, to be bestowed sometime early in life. Without getting into the weeds of funding—as J.M. Keynes said, "Anything we can do, we can afford"—the first place to look is inheritance taxes, land value taxes, and wealth taxes that will erode concentrated wealth.

A final policy I want to consider for power-sharing is the public option economy. A public option is a service provided directly by the government as an alternative to similar services available on the market. The post office, public schools, and government-funded science are examples. Arguably public libraries are another in that they provide books, media, internet access, and simple public space that would otherwise have to be rented. A public option in healthcare grants economically advantageous scale and universal coverage. Public option banking provides basic financial services to the underbanked without usurious interest rates or hassle. Public options in social media could provide an alternative to networks and algorithms that profit by manipulating our personal data and behavioral patterns.

Even if various fees and taxes (nothing is free) are involved, the purpose is not profit but public service. The idea isn't necessarily to replace private provision, which has its own advantages, but to provide an alternative, explicitly in the public interest with universal access central to the mission. Not every industry needs a public option—far from it. We can shape the public option economy with a mix of the economist's usual bag of tools—market efficiency, public goods, externalities, and the like—with democratic feedback. As several of the examples above suggest, public options are often popular, and very often taken for granted to the point of people forgetting there's something called a "public option" at all.

It's fair to ask how so-called liberal socialism is really socialism at all, rather than just another reformist left-liberalism. One answer is simply that there is no hard difference between liberal socialism and left-liberalism, no magical moment where reform transforms into revolution. But I hope it's becoming clear how a naïve "social ownership of the means of production" definition of socialism is met—from a certain point of view. First, like many liberals have held from the beginning, property rights are not absolute. They are socially determined and must ultimately bend to social purposes. Second, unlike many liberals, we see economic inequality as a serious danger to a free democracy that demands direct policy attention. Third, basic incomes and asset grants literally socialise the income and wealth of society, turning the means of production into a source of rents for all. And the public option economy socialises parts of the economy without the destructive consequences of central planning.

Okay, Liberal.

Yet liberal socialism remains unmistakably liberal, even capitalist. If we take the dreaded c-word to indicate an economic system where there is private ownership of business and capital and these private owners pursue profit, then it's consistent with everything written above, and there is no fundamental contradiction between capitalism and socialism.

But this needlessly needles the left. Surely if it is anything at all, capitalism is a political system that favors the interests of capitalists. Fine, then liberal socialism will maintain an entrepreneurial market economy. We keep this system because it delivers the goods—at scale. As liberals, we're right to emphasize this, even while as socialists we emphasize the state's entrepreneurial research and engineering efforts. These are complementary, not oppositional. The kind of society Marx imagined, where work would no longer be bled out of human beings by the cruel lash of necessity, can only rise out of the abundance—green, of course—of a liberal market order.

Liberal markets are also a matter of personal freedom. Trading, bartering, saving, buying, and selling—of even our labor—is something humans are naturally predisposed to, and the attempt to suppress these dispositions tends to lead to violence and oppression. Bettering our condition and that of our families and loved ones is likewise natural and salubrious.

Most socialists have no particular allergy to markets as such—Bernie Sanders and Alexandria Ocasio-Cortez are on a Fight Oligarchy tour, not an Abolish Markets tour. So it's worth spelling out the market's humanistic value. The market is a place where people from all kinds of backgrounds, nationalities, and religions come together in peace for the express purpose of fulfilling each other's needs and desires. The market economy is an extended order of peaceful co-operation. When exploitative conditions and relations of domination are barred from taking hold, there's nothing left for the socialist but to celebrate the diversity and creativity of the market.

But the market in a large commercial society like ours is also a place to find oneself. There are many more varieties of employment and diversion in the cosmopolitan commercial society than in the tribe or commune, more opportunities to, as it were, fish, hunt, herd, and criticize, just as you like. There too are more fashions, cuisines, disciplines, and niche interests on display.

Solidarity, identity politics, antifascism—but I repeat myself.

Along with the dazzling difference that accompanies commercial modernity come opportunities for the privileged and powerful to exploit those differences, turning against one another people whose rational interests and values should align. Exploiting wedges between people is how power and inequality entrench themselves. Solidarity, the key social virtue of socialism, requires reaching across social differences and standing together against the narratives and ideologies that justify privilege and divide the laboring classes.

The contours of inequality and oppression differ from one society to another based on their own historical contingencies. In America, antiblack racism shapes life outcomes from the racial wealth gap and incarceration rates to maternal mortality and life expectancies. It also profoundly shapes politics, providing the animating force behind both political parties, their respective agendas, and their compromises with each other. Much of the late-twentieth-century conservative movement in the US can be understood as a backlash against the greater inclusion achieved by the civil rights movement, just as Jim Crow can only be understood as a backlash against Reconstruction, and MAGA as the same spirit of slavery reasserting itself in response to the advent of the first black president.

Patriarchy is an even older and more powerful obstacle to solidarity and egalitarian freedom than race. It artificially divides labor into masculine and feminine categories and extracts the latter (reproductive labor, domestic labor, and the care of children and the infirm) almost always without financial reward. Patriarchy shapes the kinds of personal and economic lives both men and women can lead, offering leadership to men and lower-paying, lower-prestige jobs to women. Patriarchy even adapts to lower the relative wages and esteem of professions when women begin to move into them in large numbers.

Misogyny punishes women who step out of acceptable social positions, with insults and character assassinations lobbed at women who seek positions of authority or who challenge the moral standing of men. This has world-shifting political force. As the modern economy has evolved toward more service-sector and office jobs, and away from jobs requiring more sweat and sinew, women across the rich world have found themselves able to advance in social standing and economic independence—many no longer need men in any economic sense. This has resulted in a global backlash that has opened up the hearts and minds of men to once fringe reactionary political movements that promise to return men to a nostalgic world where women (and disfavored minorities) treated men with the respect they believe is their birthright. These movements would rather burn democracy to the ground than counsel young men to engage women as independent equals.

These reactionary movements always involve anti-immigrant politics. Immigrants are the human symbol of changing society, and change is portrayed as the problem. This is the root of the matter. The bad economic arguments and concern-trolling about immigrant culture are just fig leaves to cover the feeling that immigrants are taking away from white men the society that once belonged to them without question.

For any liberal socialism to succeed at reining in inequality, it has to tackle the particular obstacles confronting different groups in society. In the case of racism, that may mean reparations or affirmative action. Ignoring race or pretending at "colorblindness" in favor of some imagined proletariat untouched by racial politics can only cede narrative framing to rightwing parties ready and willing to appeal to racial resentment. For women, that may mean quotas for public office to ensure equal representation, or a public option for childcare to foster fuller participation in the economy on more equitable terms. The closed border looms over immigrants' heads like the sword of Damocles, subjecting them to the mercy of more powerful employers, landlords, and fickle voters. Only a firmly open border with a clear path to citizenship for all who desire it truly respects the immigrant as a worker and human being.

Reactionary movements are never abstract. They draw on the particular social cleavages already extant in society, the deep ravines in our collective consciousness cut by generations of resentment over race, religion, ethnicity, gender, and immigration. The parts of our brains that are constantly sizing up where we and everyone around us perch on the social ladder light up when someone acts out of place; it registers as a moral transgression. This status sensitivity informs our prejudices against disfavored groups, which take on a moral character. Gender roles and sexuality are thus thick with moral valence. Affirming the status of the privileged patriarch is a kind of piety—perverted, but no less felt in our moral senses.

Liberal socialist solidarity calls for climbing out of the ravine of resentment. Identity politics is the hard, committed work of disenchanting the moral mythologies of white male status and resisting the baleful narratives arrayed against women and minorities. Solidarity movements that try to paper over identity will always slide back down into the ravine and break apart on the rocks.

This brings us to fascism, the spiritual dead-end where these reactionary political movements lead. Fascism is the crescendo of reactionary resentment after it has discarded the niceties of democratic and liberal values. It is the political will to put women and minorities back in their place by force in order to reestablish old dominance hierarchies. Because these kinds of resentments—in gentler times the stuff of merely conservative but still democratic politics—are a human universal, the threat of fascism and its attendant horrors can never fully go away. It is not "Never again" but "It will happen again, and we must gird ourselves against the darkness."

Liberal socialism insists on an egalitarian free society—each for all and all for each. We have two nemeses: fascism—the rule of the herrenvolk patriarchs—and oligarchy—the rule of plundering plutocrats. These are timeless conflicts that sustain liberal socialism as a fighting creed, but in the present moment the fascists and the plutocrats have joined forces. Liberal socialists thus form a natural anchor for a popular front antifascist coalition. And the urgent goal is to make liberals and socialists intelligible to one another, our alliance obvious and natural.

Part II:
The Liberal SocialistCanon

THE LIBERAL SOCIALIST CANON[1]

A liberal socialist economic project thus needs to experiment with property rights actions through contract law, antitrust activity, sectoral regulation, tax policy, and other rules determining conditions of ownership and the location of economic activity to affect the organization and performance of the economy, the patterning of economic governance, the spatial distribution of economic growth, and the degree of inequality present in the economic system. It is committed to the proposition that capitalism's lock on the state and political process is not absolute and that transactions between the state and capital can be renegotiated and transformed in an egalitarian direction. This working hypothesis is confirmed, I believe, by the ferocity of the current assault by capital on so many of the rules and regulations concerning state-economy transactions. This power-grab aimed at the contraction of government and collective democratic authority and the expansion of private prerogative does more than threaten growing economic inequality; for it narrows the scope of democracy and mocks the meaning of liberal rights.

Ira Katznelson, Liberalism's Crooked Circle

---

1   Originally Printed in *Liberal Currents*.

Many of us were brought up in a cultural environment where "liberal socialism" would be taken as at best a curiosity, at worst an oxymoron. It was well understood that liberalism meant supporting individualism rather than collectivism, capitalism rather than socialism, and at least some "sensible" kinds of conservative values like respect for authority and law over and against the revolutionary values of the Left. These well-worn narratives are long overdue for serious revaluation, and fortunately are receiving it. In his recent *Liberalism Against Itself*, Samuel Moyn reminds us that liberalism came into the world as a revolutionary creed committed to liberty, equality and solidarity for all. Prior to the very late ascendancy of Cold War liberals who drew heavily on conservative themes, many important liberal thinkers not only learnt from but identified with the ambitions of radical reformers and socialists.

Elizabeth Anderson in *Hijacked* observes how liberals divided on who should receive the lion's share of the wealth in society, with those endorsing a more "conservative work ethic" arguing for the rich and others arguing for the poor. That those endorsing the "conservative work ethic" won out for a while should be little reason for taking their views as representative. Helena Rosenblatt's *The Lost History of Liberalism* goes so far as to argue that "classical liberalism" is in fact very much a recent discursive creation, as from the beginning liberals from Smith to Mill felt very strongly that much more needed to be done to help the poor. This included arguing for "liberal socialism," with luminaries like Hobhouse claiming that "true Socialism serves to complete rather than to destroy the leading Liberal ideals."

My book *The Political Theory of Liberal Socialism* is intended as a brief and by no means definitive "retrieval" of the intellectual side of this important political tradition. I argue that liberal socialists are broadly committed to three principles.

1. Methodological Collectivism and Normative Individualism: Liberal socialists believe that human beings are social animals and can only flourish in the right context. However, it is ultimately the flourishing of existing individuals (and potentially future ones) which normatively matters — not the flourishing of abstract entitles like the state or nation.

2. A Developmental rather than Acquisitive Ethic: Liberal socialists are committed to each person having as equal an opportunity to lead a good life as possible through the provision of shared resources and the design of social institutions for the co-operative development of their human powers or capacities. This developmental ethic is distinct from the extractive or acquisitive one characteristic of possessive individualism, which focuses on acquisition for the purposes of hedonic gratification or the pursuit of profit.

3. Finally, liberal socialists are committed to a basic social structure with highly participatory liberal-democratic political institutions and protections for liberal rights. Liberal socialists want to extend liberal democratic principles into the economy and the family to establish more egalitarian arrangements, free of domination and exploitation.

I call the book a "retrieval" because it doesn't offer a defense of any particular flavor of liberal socialism; or even these three core principles. Instead it just discusses some of the major figures in the tradition, their insights and weaknesses, before speculating on the future. In that vein this essay will just briefly introduce readers to some of the major liberal socialist authors and their respective positions. The hope is this will provoke further discussion and reading. Of course the list is hardly exhaustive.

Antecedents to liberal socialism

Thomas Paine

Personal property is the effect of society; and it is as impossible for an individual to acquire personal property without the aid of society, as it is for him to make land originally. Separate an individual from society, and give him an island or continent to possess, and he cannot acquire personal property. He cannot be rich... All accumulation, therefore, of personal property, beyond what a man's own hands produce derived to him by living in society; and he owes on every principle of justice, of gratitude, and of civilization, a party of that accumulation back again to society from whence the whole came.

Agrarian Justice

Thomas Paine was an enormously influential figure in two revolutions. His classic polemic against aristocracy, *Common Sense,* was widely distributed during the American Revolution. Initially he was largely committed to conventional economic views. But by the time of the second half of Paine's *Rights of Man* and "Agrarian Justice," he'd shifted notably. Here he increasingly insists that enormous concentrations of wealth are neither natural nor beneficial to society. This extends even to the culture; Paine, like Adam Smith, laments the "superstitious awe, the enslaving reverence, that formerly surrounded affluence..." He claims the rich owe the poor a significant debt for the often extravagant efforts society makes in preserving their property. Paine argues this debt can be paid off through steep redistributive policies, including: a proto-universal inheritance, old age funds, guaranteed well-renumerated work, quality public education and more. Most importantly, Paine avoids describing this in terms of charity or even generosity — the poor are entitled to this as a matter of right, and the rich cannot deny it to them without violating those rights.

Mary Wollstonecraft

Security of property! Behold, in a few words, the definition of English liberty. And to this selfish principle every nobler one is sacrificed. The Briton takes place of the man, and the image of God is lost in the citizen! But it is not that enthusiastic flame which in Greece and Rome consumed every sordid passion: no, self is the focus; and the disparting rays rise not above our foggy atmosphere. But softly — it is only the property of the rich that is secure; the man who lives by the sweat of his brow has no asylum from oppression; the strong man may enter — when was the castle of the poor sacred?

A Vindication of the Rights of Man

Mary Wollstonecraft is best known for her stirring defense of women's rights in *A Vindication of the Rights of Woman*. Less well known were her calls for equality on other fronts; notably economic. Wollstonecraft lampooned conservatives like Burke for making a fetish of property and hierarchy, even chastising them for leaning on hyper-emotional appeals to "tradition" and affection for the way things are. In *A Vindication of the Rights of Woman,* she claims that from "respect paid to property flow, as from a poisoned fountain, most of the evils and vices which render this world such a dreary scene to the contemplative mind."

Initially much of her revulsion was directed against aristocratic and inherited property. But during Wollstonecraft's travels, chronicled in her *Letters Written During a Short Residence in Sweden, Norward, and Denmark,* her venom extended to burgeoning forms of capitalism. She described capitalists as a "species of fungus" whose petty fascination with wealth inoculates them against "greatness of mind" and "embrutes them till they term all virtue of an heroic cast, romantic attempts at something above our nature, and anxiety about the welfare of others, a search after misery in which we have no concern." Unfortunately, Wollstonecraft's early death meant none of these thoughts were systematically developed.

Liberal Socialism Matures

John Stuart Mill

If some Nero or Domitian was to require a hundred persons to run a race for their lives, on condition that the fifty or twenty who came in hindmost should be put to death, it would not be any diminution that the strongest or nimblest would, except through some untoward accident, be certain to escape. The misery and the crime would be that they were put to death at all. So in the economy of society; if there be any who suffer physical privation or moral degradation ... [it] is pro tanto a failure of the social arrangements. And to assert as a mitigation of the evil that those who thus suffer are the weaker members of the community, morally or physically, is to add insult to misfortune.

Socialism

John Stuart Mill is in many respects the first comprehensive liberal socialist philosopher. In his *Autobiography* Mill notes how in his earlier years he'd seen little further than the classical political economists, before maturing sufficiently to recognize it was possible to go further than capitalism in ameliorating human misery. This led Mill to proudly identify "under the general designation of Socialists." Mill's socialism was unique in of course placing an enormous emphasis on personal liberty. He was deeply concerned with early arguments for statist and command economic approaches to socialism. But in later editions of *Principles of Political Economy*, Mill opined that capitalists really didn't contribute much of value to firms, even though they were well remunerated for their idleness. He argued for a transition to worker-managed firms in market settings — an early kind of market socialism that would be decentralized but still entail workers owning and running the means of production. This would be accompanied by redistributive public spending organized by what was a generous welfare state by nineteenth-century standards.

L.T. Hobhouse

If then, there be such a thing as a Liberal Socialism-and whether there be is still a subject for inquiry — it must clearly fulfill two conditions. In the first place, it must be democratic. It must come from below, not from above. Or rather, it must emerge from the efforts of society as a whole to secure a fuller measure of justice, and a better organization of mutual aid. It must engage the efforts and respond to the genuine desires not of a handful of superior beings, but of the great masses of men. And secondly, and for that very reason, it must make its account with the human individual. It must give the average man free play in the person life for which he really cares. It must be founded on liberty, and must make not for the suppression but for the development of the personality.

Liberalism

L.T. Hobhouse is less read than some of these others, which is a shame. While he was not an original thinker on par with Wollstonecraft, Mill or Rawls, Hobhouse was a powerful synthesist with a knack for clear exposition. Like Paine and Mill, he makes fun of the idea that "wealth" and "property" are natural and not social phenomena.

[The] prosperous business man who thinks that he has made his fortunate entirely by self help does not pause to consider what single strep he could have taken on the road to his success but for the ordered tranquility which has made commercial development possible, the security by road, and rail, and seas, the masses of skilled labour, and the sum of intelligence which civilization has placed at his disposal, the very demand for the goods which he produces which the general progress of the world has created, the inventions which he uses as a matter of course and which have been built up by the collective effort of generations of men of science and organizers of industry.

This means society is an "indispensable partner" to the creation of the rich man's riches. Hobhouse notes how these kind of meritocratic mythologies aren't harmless when they offer ideological justifications for inequality and a lack of economic democracy. He emphasized how great inequalities result in them ceasing to be "essentially an institution by which each man can secure to himself the fruits of his own labour, and become an instrument whereby the owner can command the labour of others on terms which he is in general able to dictate." The solution had to be establishing a society where the needs of all were met.

Eduard Bernstein

It is indeed true that the great liberal movement of modern times has, in the first instance, benefited the capitalist bourgeoisie, and that the parties which took the name Liberal were, or became in time, nothing but straightforward defenders of capitalism. There can, of course, be nothing but enmity between these parties and Social Democracy. But with respect to liberalism as a historical movement, socialism is its legitimate heir, not only chronologically, but also intellectually. Moreover, this receives practical confir-

mation in every question of principle on which Social Democracy has had to take a stand. Whenever an economic demand in the socialist programme was to be met in a manner, or under circumstances, which appeared seriously to endanger the development of freedom, Social Democracy has never shied away from opposing it. For Social Democracy, the defense of civil liberty has always taken precedence over the fulfillment of any economic postulate. The aim of all socialist measures, even of those that outwardly appear to be coercive measures, is the development and protection of the free personality.

The Preconditions of Socialism

Eduard Bernstein is an important thinker whose work has recently been reintroduced by Elizabeth Anderson and Gary Dorrien, among others. In his day Bernstein was enormously controversial for arguing that socialism could be achieved through reform rather than direct revolution. He also wrote respectfully about Marx, while being critical of orthodox Marxism's emphasis on economic determinism and ignoring problems with the labor theory of value. Bernstein argued that the movement to socialism would be a process rather than a break with liberalism. Indeed, he claimed that socialism was very much the "heir" of liberalism as an Enlightenment doctrine committed to securing liberty, equality and solidarity for all, politically and economically. For Bernstein, one could even "call socialism 'organized liberalism,' for if we examine more closely the organization that socialism wants, and how it wants them, we will find that what primarily distinguishes them from the superficially similar feudal institutions is their liberalism: their democratic constitution and openness." During the First World War, he found himself at the center of further controversies for refusing to endorse the conflict and later highlight German responsibility for helping launch the war. None the less, he later became one of the chief reference points of movements arguing for democratic socialism and social democracy.

Carlo Rosselli

Socialism is nothing more than the logical development, taken to its extreme consequences, of the principle of liberty. Socialism, when understood in its fundamental sense and judged by its results — as the concrete movement for the emancipation of the proletariat — is liberalism in action; it means that liberty comes into the life of poor people. Socialism says the abstract recognition of liberty of conscience and political freedoms for all, though it may represent an essential moment in the development of political theory, is a thing of very limited value when the majority of men, forced to live as a result of circumstances of birth and environment in moral and material poverty, are left without the possibility of appreciating its significance and taking any actual advantage of it. Liberty without the accompaniment and support of a minimum of economic autonomy, without emancipation from the grip of pressing material necessity, does not exist for the individual; it is a mere phantasm.

Liberal Socialism

Carlo Rosselli never had time or opportunity to produce a grand scholarly work on liberal socialism. The book which bears that title was written in part while Rosselli was being jailed by the Italian Fascist party. He later escaped and died fighting for the Republican cause in the Spanish Civil War. Like Bernstein, Rosselli is critical of what he takes to be deterministic and mechanical versions of Marxism — perhaps to a fault. Rosselli argues for integrating socialist and liberal principles together; an aspiration he thinks should be natural given their abiding alignment on many issues. That many liberals disagreed owes much to their having become "dogmatic" in defending "economic libertarianism" while failing to recognize how the forms of domination that emerge under capitalism limit the liberty of the poor. One way to offset this is the "constitutionalization of the factor regime" where workers should enjoy greater basic rights, including to democratic control. A very brave man with a forceful style, it's a great tragedy that Rosselli's life and contributions were cut by combat with the authoritarian right.

C.B. Macpherson

The notion that individualism and 'collectivism' are the opposite ends of a scale along which states and theories of the state can be arranged, regardless of the stage of social development in which they appear, is superficial and misleading. Locke's individualism, that of an emerging capitalist society, does not exclude but on the contrary demands the supremacy of the state over the individual. It is not a question of the more thorough-going the individualism, the less collectivism; rather the more thorough-going the individualism, the more complete the collectivism.

The Political Theory of Possessive Individualism

C.B. Macpherson was a Canadian political theorist best known for his critique of "possessive" forms of individualism, which he argued provided an ideological foundation for classical liberal and neoliberal defenses of capitalism. These "possessive" commitments underpinned societies characterized by capitalist domination. But Macpherson also argued there were forms of liberalism worthy of "retrieval." This included the forms of Left-liberalism defended by figures like Mill, which dropped many of the ideological mythologies about property being natural and hard work being the basis of reward. Instead they focused on envisioning societies where a "developmental" ethic would replace an "acquisitive" one, and the development of each person's human powers became the end of social and political policy. Such a developmental liberalism would need to be paired with an extension of democracy into the economy and an erosion of plutocratic political forces.

John Rawls

Welfare state capitalism also rejects the fair value of the political liberties, and while it has some concern for equality of opportunity, the policies necessary to achieve that are not followed. It permits very large inequalities in the ownership of real property (productive assets and natural resources) so that the control of the economy and much of political life rests in few hands. And although, as the name 'welfare-state capitalism' suggest, welfare provisions may be quite generous and guarantee a decent social minimum covering the basic needs, a principle of reciprocity to regulate economic and social inequalities is not recognized ... This leaves... property owning democracy and liberal socialism: their ideal descriptions include arrangements designed to satisfy the two principles of justice.

Justice as Fairness: A Restatement

If Mill was the most important liberal thinker of the nineteenth century, Rawls was the most important liberal thinker of the twentieth. It is quite telling that the two most important liberal thinkers of two centuries either argued that only socialism could realize the aspirations of liberalism or expressed enormous sympathy for it. Rawls' *Theory of Justice* was often taken to be a defense of the mid-century welfare state. He later rejected that interpretation, holding that welfare states still permitted too many inequalities, especially economic inequalities that fed into unequal political power. Rawls argued that only a property-owning democracy or liberal socialist regime could satisfy his two principles of justice.

In the *Lectures on Political Philosophy*, Rawls rejects command economic socialism while defending the importance of learning from Marx. He calls liberal socialism an "illuminating and worthwhile view" with four key elements: 1) a constitutional democratic political regime, with the fair value of the political liberties, 2) a system of competitive markets, ensured by law as necessary, 3) a scheme of worker-owned business, or, in part, also public-owned through stock shares and managed by elected firm-chosen managers, 4) a property system establishing a widespread and a more or less even distribution of the means of production and natural resources. These Rawlsian arguments for liberal socialism have proven influential on contemporary thinkers like William Edmundson, Elizabeth Anderson, Daniel Chandler and more.

Modern Liberal Socialism

Chantal Mouffe

What is important, whatever the name, is the recognition that 'democracy' is the hegemonic signifier around which the diverse struggles are articulated and that political liberalism is not discarded. An appropriate term could be "liberal socialism" by which Norberto Bobbio refers to a social formation that combines liberal-democratic institutions and an economic framework with several socialist characteristics... Envisaged in such a way, the project of the radicalization of democracy shares some characteristics with social democracy before its conversion to social liberalism, but it is not a simple return to the postwar compromise between capital and labour.

For A Left Populism

The Belgian political theorist Chantal Mouffe has been arguing for an agonistic form of liberal socialism for many decades now. In this she is deeply inspired by the Italian thinker Norberto Bobbio, who published influential revaluations of the relationship between liberalism and socialism throughout the late twentieth century. Mouffe's own liberal socialism is far more political than the others'. She argues that countering the hegemony of reactionary movements will mean organizing a "populist" Left aligned by commitments to democratize many different areas of life. Mouffe claims this will mean "political liberalism" must be rescued from "economic liberalism" through a realization that we cannot have a society of free equal citizens where capitalism is dominant. Influenced by Carl Schmitt and others, she encourages liberal socialism to not be afraid of a language of opposition to "enemies" or radical rhetoric. While her programme is relatively unspecified, Mouffe provides valuable insights into the politics behind the political theory of liberal socialism.

Charles Mills

Black radical liberalism is a liberalism informed by the realities of racial capitalism and self-consciously oriented accordingly by the need to rethink white liberal theory in that light. So it is not merely a matter of arguing for a left/social-democratic/"socialist" liberalism, mindful of the failures of both free-market/neoliberal capitalism and Stalinist "socialism" (a familiar enough project by now), but of taking into account liberalism's historic complicity with white supremacy, both nationally and internationally.

W.E.B. Du Bois: Black Radical Liberal

Charles Mills passed away recently, meaning we unfortunately never got a systematic exposition of his "black radical liberalism." In the 1990s Mills wrote the classic polemic *The Racial Contract,* where he argued that liberal thinkers had largely ignored or actively sidelined an engagement with liberalism's racist history. This included looking at the racism of central figures in the canon like Locke, Jefferson, Kant and more. This critique continued up to late works like *Black Rights/White Wrongs*.

But in his book and later papers, Mills took a more constructive line. Drawing on the writings of people like Kant, Rawls and Tommie Shelby, Mills sought to develop a black radical liberalism which would take racism seriously and ask how liberal societies could address it more comprehensively. This included looking at the legacy of "racial capitalism" by incorporating, among other things, Marxist insights. Discussing black radical liberalism's approach to the economy, Mills notes it would "obviously be of a left-wing variety." He goes on to note that liberalism is "opposed to state-commandist socialism (what was represented as 'Communism'), but state-commandist socialism has proved itself to be a historical failure, both economically and morally. Liberalism is not in principles opposed to social democracy or market socialism."

A long and prestigious tradition

As mentioned, this list is by no means intended to be exhaustive. It doesn't include important figures discussed in *The Political Theory of Liberal Socialism* like J.M. Keynes, R.H. Tawney, Axel Honneth, and Bobbio himself. Also not discussed are other significant figures who argued for liberal socialist fusions like Paul Tillich, John Dewey and arguably Martin Luther King.

What does the future hold for liberal socialism as a theoretical and practical tradition? As a theoretical tradition, the future looks very bright indeed. Some of the most exciting work on Left-liberalism and liberal socialism is being down by historians like Moyn and Rosenblatt, philosophers like Anderson, Shelby and Edmundson, and economists like Dan Chandler and Crotty. There is a deepening sense, to paraphrase Alexandre Lefebvre, that neoliberalism has faltered for a reason. Indeed, far from being an embodiment of liberal principles, it is more like a kind of "liberaldom" that professes adherence to those principles while bastardizing what they stand for through enabling inequality and plutocracy. Whether these theoretical developments will translate into practice is hard to say. There are a lot of cliches and bad history that would have to be overcome to make a liberal socialist movement effective. But as the canon discussed here shows, liberal socialism is a long and prestigious tradition which is worthy of our attention. It offers a liberal vision that warrants not just loyalty but love.

WAS JOHN STUART MILL, SOCIALIST?[1]

John Stuart Mill was the most influential liberal thinker of the nineteenth century. Many of his arguments for free speech and personal autonomy became staples of the tradition, and he still enjoys a pious following among libertarians and self-styled classical liberals. Naturally, the latter affinity has won Mill plenty of enemies on the Left. Karl Marx famously dismissed the "imbecile flatness" of bourgeois hacks like Mill in the first volume of *Capital*. Years later, Herbert Marcuse (rightly) chided him for holding "elitist" opinions.

This is unfortunate since, as Mill put it in *Autobiography*, his "ideal of ultimate improvement went far beyond Democracy, and would class [him] decidedly under the general designation of Socialists." It doesn't get more emphatic than that.

By the end of his life, Mill espoused what we'd now call liberal socialism: a political order that protects and expands most classical liberal freedoms, but jettisons the stringent private property rights so dear to early liberals like John Locke and James Madison.

Mill's brand of liberal socialism was analytically blinkered and, in some important respects — particularly on

---

1   Reprinted from *Jacobin Magazine*.

the question of democratization — deeply flawed. But it's striking that the alleged patron saint of Victorian capitalism was in fact one of its sharpest critics.

J.S. Mill's Arguments for Liberal Socialism

By his own admission, Mill came late to socialism. Born in 1806, he was radicalized both by reading socialists like Charles Fourier and Robert Owen and by the influence of his longtime friend and eventual wife, Harriet Taylor, who pushed him to take the oppression of women and the laboring classes more seriously.

Mill's most significant writings on the subject were later editions of *The Principles of Political Economy*, the short tract *Socialism*, and *Autobiography*. Together, they showcased Mill's deepening sympathy for socialist reforms and a conviction that those who "at present [receive] the least share" of society's benefits deserve far more.

In *Socialism* he lambasted classical liberals — the "levellers of former times" — for criticizing aristocratic privilege and inherited power while failing to examine the many ways capitalist society erected similar inequalities. He praised socialists as their "far-sighted successors" — more consistent in seeking to ensure material equality as a prerequisite for the flourishing and freedom of all.

Mill's arguments for socialism were very different from the historical materialism of someone like Marx. Characterized by straightforward moral claims in the manner of the utopian socialists, Mill's politics were an intriguing mix of three distinct elements: classical liberalism, utilitarianism, and English romanticism.

From the classical liberals, Mill took a deep respect for individualism and the priority of personal liberty, while severing it from the "possessive individualism" of someone like Locke, who believed property owners had a natural right to profit from workers' labor. Mill's individualism was far more egalitarian. He retained the utilitarianism of his youth — "everybody [is] to count for one, nobody for more than one," in Jeremy Bentham's words — which established moral and material equality as the baseline from which deviations had to be justified.

But Mill was also deeply concerned that Bentham's reasoning was unduly mechanical, reducing humans to little more than hedonistic utility maximizers. So, from English romanticism, he took the position that what is important in life is not just the pursuit of pleasure, but that each is empowered to become the kind of person they wish to be — that we have the capacity to follow our "inward forces" and express our individuality through ever more diverse experiments in living.

What we get in Mill, then, is an egalitarian, expressive individualism that departs sharply from Locke in holding that all individuals must be guaranteed the ability to live good lives — not just property owners, who become rich by living off the alienated labor of workers.

Mill drew on these philosophical convictions to argue that capitalist society was fundamentally flawed. While its material productivity was undeniable, he thought capitalism failed badly in equitably distributing resources — and that it lent itself to neo-Lockean apologias about the virtues of hardworking capitalists and the vices of the poor.

Mill would have none of that. To his great credit, he recognized that most of the reasons people fall behind in capitalist society have little to do with their personal efforts — and that even if capitalists were in fact more capable and harder working, it wouldn't justify allowing millions to languish in poverty.

Writing in *Socialism*, Mill offered a scathing account of this kind of reasoning, invoking the most autocratic ancient tyrants.

If some Nero or Domitian was to require a hundred persons to run a race for their lives, on condition that the fifty or twenty who came in hindmost should be put to death, it would not be any diminution that the strongest or nimblest would, except through some untoward accident, be certain to escape. The misery and the crime would be that they were put to death at all. So in the economy of society; if there be any who suffer physical privation or moral degradation... [it] is pro tanto a failure of the social arrangements. And to assert as a mitigation of the evil that those who thus suffer are the weaker members of the community, morally or physically, is to add insult to misfortune.

The Limitations of Mill's Socialism

Mill concluded *Socialism* by arguing that a just liberal society must experiment with different types of socialist organization to better the situation of the least well-off. He never produced a systematic work explaining what those experiments should be, but in the later editions of *Principles of Political Economy* he endorsed worker co-operatives as superior to capitalist-managed firms and insisted there was "nothing in principle in economic theory" that spoke against experimenting with socialist principles and forms of organization. He also argued the state should help secure more equal economic opportunities for all and supply an array of public services, particularly education.

Interestingly, he was one of the first major liberal and socialist writers to take seriously the problem of women's equality and, in "The Subjection of Women," even wrote that reform must go beyond securing liberal political rights for women. Patriarchal institutions like the family, he wrote, would have to be scrutinized and refashioned.

His record was less admirable on the question of democracy. Mill had some democratic instincts, arguing for universal suffrage in *Considerations on Representative Government* and, as a member of parliament, calling for the enfranchisement of not just working-class men but women as well. Some of his concerns with democratic rule — for instance, the potential for a tyrannical majority to oppress minorities — remain valid.

But he was also trepidatious about the uneducated and unintelligent having too much of a say in politics, and supported British colonialism, viewing the non-European subjects of its empire with condescension. He didn't seem to grasp how the persistence of parochial attitudes and institutions maintained the inequalities he frequently criticized.

This speaks to the second major limitation of Mill's liberal socialism: its lackluster interpretation of power. Mill stuck to making ethical arguments for liberal socialism. Undeniably convinced it was the right social arrangement, he viewed moral suasion as the means to bring it about. He seemed doggedly uninterested in analyzing the power dynamics of the bourgeois liberal state, its history, and the way imperial powers like the United Kingdom worked to spread capitalism at the barrel of a gun. He failed to think through what social agents might have the power and interest in winning a liberal socialist order.

Mill was aware that concentrating political power in the hands of capital and the wealthy undercuts egalitarian reforms, and he even recognized that seemingly private institutions, like the patriarchal family, are defined by unequal power dynamics that require correction. But he was simply unwilling to contemplate a more thorough democratization of society, even though it could break up many coercive power structures.

On these points, someone like Marx is simply a far more acute and helpful analyst than Mill.

The Value of Mill

Mill was a complex thinker who was often tugged in multiple directions. Rather than choosing a path and sticking to it, his response was usually to try to synthesize the best elements of competing traditions into a seamless whole. Nowhere is this clearer than in his variant of liberal socialism, which linked liberalism's commitments to individualism and moral equality to the socialist demands for economic equality and workplace democracy.

Any liberal socialism today would need to be more throughgoing in its democratic commitments and shrewder in its analysis of power in capitalist societies. But Mill does provide a platform for thinking more carefully about the relationship between the great modernist doctrines of liberalism and socialism, and how they might be conciliated.

At the very least, those of us on the Left shouldn't allow libertarians and classical liberals to claim him as one of their own when Mill called himself a socialist and heaped nothing but scorn on defenders of capitalist exploitation and inequality.

So...two cheers for J.S. Mill?

THE LEFT SHOULD RECLAIM JOHN RAWLS' THEORY OF JUSTICE[1]

John Rawls is widely considered one of — if not *the* — most influential among American philosophers. Rawls's work, and work on his work, has been cited thousands of times. He was awarded the National Humanities Medal by president Bill Clinton (one of the few commendable decisions Clinton ever made), and there is a veritable library's worth of introductory guides and YouTube explainers on his work.

Rawls's academic influence has been so pronounced that political philosophers across the spectrum have either written long critiques of his work or tried to show how, say, Marxism is compatible with his theory of justice as fairness. This even though Rawls was legendarily modest and not a particularly good writer — not to mention that Rawls's thinking never obtained the interdisciplinary sweep of his libertarian rival Robert Nozick or contemporary political philosophers like Martha Nussbaum or Jürgen Habermas.

Despite these achievements, Rawls is an odd and even, in a way, tragic figure. For a long time, his magnum opus, *A Theory of Justice*, was rather crudely praised or condemned

---

1   Reprinted from *Jacobin Magazine*.

as offering the most systematic defense of the mid-twentieth-century liberal welfare state. While this seriously understated his radicalism, the irony is that even this moderate welfarism was being rolled back by the time Rawls published *Theory* in 1971.

Richard Nixon's paper-thin victory in 1968 was the harbinger of the conservative turn that would begin in the 1970s and kick into cocaine-fueled high gear in the "Greed Is Good" '80s. By the 1990s, the same Bill Clinton who gave Rawls a medal was also declaring that the "era of Big Government" was over and was competing with Republicans to see who could put more minorities in jail faster. By most accounts, Rawls was aware that the United States was becoming a less and less just society, and there is a feeling of gloomy resignation in his later books, like *Justice as Fairness* (2001).

Yet the generations that have grown up witnessing regular major recessions in 2008 and 2020 have begun rediscovering Rawls's work and putting it to the more radical purposes it was intended for. This makes the new collection *Rawls's A Theory of Justice at 50*, edited by Paul Weithman, a welcome contribution.

Reintroducing John Rawls

I identify as a liberal socialist academic. So *Rawls's A Theory of Justice at 50* is very much a book for readers like myself.

It is very much an academic volume, and surveys a range of scholarly views on Rawlsian philosophy. It includes contributions from well-known philosophers, including Elizabeth Anderson, Samuel Scheffler, Samuel Freeman, and Joshua Cohen. Given this, potential readers should be warned that this is most definitely not an introductory volume; an extensive background in his major works and the debates around it is presupposed. But the book does take time to showcase the power of Rawlsian philosophy to address real-world problems and even manages to be inspirational at points (a rare feat for texts analytic on philosophy).

It's tough to review a collection of essays on a major thinker since each author brings their own interests and specialities to bear. This means that a reader will naturally gravitate to the essays that most align with their own interests, and that was very much the case with me: the essays that grabbed my attention most were those on economic and racial justice, along with the quite moving concluding paper on how Rawls speaks to contemporary political problems.

David Brudney's "The *Theory* Rawls, the 1844 Marx, and the Market" stresses the overlap between the young Karl Marx's humanist critique of capitalism and Rawls's criticism. Brudney points out how both authors were deeply sensitive to how the competitive ethos generated by capitalist markets could corrode ties of solidarity and undermine the social bases for the working classes' self-respect — particularly by broiling alienation, indifference, and rivalry. The essay is tantalizingly short, and even Brudney admits that the tale he "wants to tell is a long one. Unfortunately...it has to be several compressed."

But he is surely onto something with this analysis. Books like Rodney Peffer's *Marxism, Morality, and Social Justice* and the more recent *Beyond Liberal Egalitarianism* by Tony Smith have shown the power and creativity of Rawls/ Marx fusions. Hopefully Brudney decides to take his compressed tale and turn it into an epic. Elizabeth Anderson's "Rawls's Principles of Justice as a Transcendence of Class Warfare" sees her taking the socialist tradition increasingly seriously. I still think her analysis would benefit from some infusions of Marxist dialectics, particularly regarding the forms of domination that are specific to capital. In *Mute*

Compulsion, Marxist philosopher Søren Mau reminds us that it is peculiar to capitalist society that power operates in the three different forms of direct coercion, ideological manipulation, and the imposition of market imperatives on both workers and bosses. A comparable analysis would enrich the account of power in the Rawlsian tradition Anderson works in.

Nevertheless, her situating Rawls in relation to Ricardian, Fabian, and Christian socialism fills in important history. And her argument that Rawls's "principles of justice attempt to end class society by preventing inequalities in income, wealth, education and occupation from consolidating into distinct and heritable class identities" provides one of the clearest expositions yet on why the "welfarist" view of Rawls was simply wrong.

More painful reflections on Rawls's legacy are provided by papers from Henry Richardson and Tommie Shelby on the question of race. Inspired by the late great Charles Mills, both Richardson and Shelby affirm that Rawls was unjustly silent on matters of racial oppression and the extent to which white supremacist doctrines continued to permeate American society as systematic racism. These charges hit home, and they demonstrate the extent to which Rawls's ideal-theoretic approach to political philosophy needed to be more attentive to material relations of power and history.

Richardson and Shelby argue that Rawls's approach can be rescued as a theoretic weapon against racism by reconfiguring core ideas like the "original position" to take account of the history of racial oppression. I agree, but would add that Rawlsian moral theory will be fundamentally incomplete without a systematic critical theory to complement it. Black radical Marxism à la Cedric J. Robinson would be an especially helpful supplement, as would the decades of critiques of neoliberalism by authors from Wendy Brown to Quinn Slobodian.

The Enduring Relevance of *A Theory of Justice*

We may reject the contention that the ordering of institutions is always defective because the distribution of natural talents and the contingencies of social circumstance are unjust, and this injustice must inevitably carry over to human arrangements. Occasionally this reflection is offered as an excuse for ignoring injustice, as if the refusal to acquiesce in injustice is on a par with being unable to accept death. The natural distribution is neither just nor unjust; nor is it unjust that persons are born into society at some particular position. These are simply natural facts. What is just and unjust is the way that institutions deal with these facts.

John Rawls, A Theory of Justice

My favorite paper in the collection was the very last one: "A Society of Self-Respect" by Leif Wenar. Analytic philosophy, including Rawls, has an unfortunately deserved reputation for floating above the particularities of actual political controversies. Wenar gestures to this when he points out how even though Rawls occupies the ninth circle of academic heaven, very few of his core ideas have trickled down into the public culture. Ask anyone on the street where the idea of "class conflict" comes from and they'll say Marx, and most people think of Friedrich Nietzsche when they hear "God is dead!" But despite its analytical simplicity as a thought experiment, even most very educated people could probably not tell you what the "original position" was all about.

Wenar thinks this is a real shame, since the rise of right-wing populism in the United States and abroad showcases why Rawls's ideas are so necessary. As he puts it, many members of the white working class voted for Donald

Trump as a middle finger to the establishment. While misguided, their reaction is at least partially the fault of centrist liberals and technocrats who long ago gave up the idea of a fighting liberalism that centers the least well-off. Wenar ends by imagining a conversation with an Uber driver in a Rawlsian society who is proud of how his country is a fair place where inequality is largely a thing of the past and the least well-off in society are at the center of our political concerns.

It's a beautiful vision, rendered haunting by the contrast with our current neoliberal regime, characterized by both complacent centrists and surging authoritarian populists. Reading *Rawls's A Theory of Justice at 50* appropriately makes one think back to all the major social and political developments of the past fifty years. The conclusion is a grim one: the United States has moved further and further away from being a just society and has helped drag much of the world with it.

Since the heyday of the already inadequate liberal welfare state, we've endured generations of neoliberal governments claiming the banner of liberalism for themselves. Under its auspices, they pushed policies that rolled back welfare for the most vulnerable, decreased union density and undercut the labor movement, backed neoconservative imperialists in their illegal wars, and advanced carceral measures as mechanisms to ameliorate social discontent. The result is a cruel society where the ruling orders largely feel they owe little to anyone, and where the working and lower classes are made to feel responsible for their own subordination.

As Samuel Moyn has chronicled, the liberalism that Rawls defended (as a radical ideology that prioritized the interests of the least well-off) drank ever deeper from the well of conservative thought — becoming skeptical, wary, and unhopeful. We've all enjoyed the dark fruit of this failure of imagination and will for too long.

Rawls tells us justice is the first virtue of social institutions, as truth is to systems of thought. Our society is not just or virtuous — but it could be if we rediscovered the courage to make the world anew. Taking Rawls's own ideas seriously, and attempting to apply them to the real-world problems of our time, may be a good place to start.

C.B. MACPHERSON ON RETRIEVING LIBERAL RADICALISM[1]

Left-liberalism is having a moment. The last few weeks and months have seen the publication of a wide array of generally high-quality books, articles, and commentary. A short list includes Samuel Moyn's *Liberalism Against It self*, Elizabeth Anderson's *Hijacked: How Neoliberalism Turned the Work Ethic Against Workers and How Workers Can Take It Back*, Dan Chandler's *Free And Equal*, and Helen McCabe's *John Stuart Mill: Socialist*, alongside forthcoming books by Alexandre Lefebvre and myself. Much of this is a response to the widespread acknowledgement that liberalism has now spent a decade in crisis; though who the villains are in this saga is debated.

For right-wing liberals like George Will or Jonah Goldberg, the enemies are radicals to the Left and hard Right who threaten the ordered liberty/classical liberal tradition they claim has served liberalism well. For Left-liberals, the answer becomes considerably more complicated. Right-wing authoritarianism is the main danger to be confronted. But Left-liberals accept that winning this battle will require liberalism first win a battle within,

---

1   Reprinted from *Liberal Currents*.

through soul-searching for what went wrong and why. How did liberalism, at least in its post-1980s neoliberal form, go from being the winning ideological contender atop the end of history to seeing monthly prognoses of its demise?

Understanding where liberalism stepped wrong requires a look back at its history, and there are few better guides for Left-liberals than C.B. Macpherson. Macpherson was well known not long ago as one of the twentieth century's premiere political theorists. A professor at the University of Toronto, he had a loyal following, including future stars of Canadian politics like the late NDP leader Ed Broadbent. However, times changed, and for a while it seemed like Macpherson's work had become passé in a world where right-wing liberals were destined to be forever ascendant.

There has been a considerable resurgence of interest in his work by scholars like Frank Cunningham, Philip Hansen, and Igor Shoikhedbrod. It is not hard to understand why. Being best known for his pioneering critique of "possessive individualism" in the classical liberal tradition led many to identify Macpherson with Marxism-though he never explicitly embraced the label. Less well known is Macpherson's longer-term project of "retrieval" — his attempt to recover a more emancipatory and egalitarian core to the liberal tradition which was worth carrying on in a more humane society. Left-liberals and liberal socialists in the twenty-first century have much to learn from his pioneering efforts to show where liberalism went awry and where the possibilities of repairing it lie. For Macpherson, "retrieving" what is best in the liberal tradition means taking seriously classical liberalism's principled commitments to equality and liberty for all, but realizing they can't be successfully instantiated in a competitive, possessive society. Though what society could instantiate them is unclear from his work.

Macpherson on classical liberalism's promise

Macpherson's magnum opus is his 1962 book *The Political Theory of Possessive Individualism*. The text's relatively modest explicit ambition is dwarfed by its impact. A historical study of English political theory in the seventeenth century (running the gamut from Hobbes to Locke) shouldn't make waves, yet the implications are extraordinary. Macpherson explains many of the core assumptions and prejudices that were baked into the classical liberal tradition, even where he acknowledges its obvious improvement on past ideas. Macpherson notes how early liberal thought was distinctive in emphasizing a principle of human equality, which in turn bequeathed liberal notions of equal basic rights and liberties.

This was radically different from antiquarian thought, which had often taken for granted the basic inequity of human beings. Leo Strauss noted this fact in *The City and Man* when he pointed out that for Aristotle (and other ancient thinkers):

> political inequality is ultimately justified by the natural inequality among men. The fact that some men are by nature rulers and others by nature ruled points to the inequality pervading nature as a whole: the whole as an ordered whole consists of beings of different rank.

This argument for political and natural inequality came under serious pressure with the advent of Stoic and Christian philosophy, which militated against its elitism by stressing the common mortality and sinfulness of human beings.

But as Macpherson notes, it was liberal thinkers who successfully mobilized around ideals of equality, enacting revolutionary ideological and structural changes, beginning with Hobbes, who mocked Aristotelian and ancient pretensions to assert unequal right between unequals. Macpherson points out that Hobbes' insistence on radical physical and moral equality between individuals was a "leap in political theory as radical as Galileo's formulation of the law of uniform motion was in natural science, and not unrelated to it." Hobbes reconceived human beings as essentially material and mechanical creatures who were not subject to rights and obligations imposed by some outside teleological force. Human beings had to assess their "own requirements" so there

> could be no question of imposing a system of values from outside or above. Hence there could be no question of finding a hierarchy of wants or of rights or of obligations. Everyone's must be assumed to be equal. It was Hobbes refusal to impose moral difference on men's wants, his acceptance of the equal need for continued motion as the sufficient source of rights, that constituted his revolution in moral and political theory. Hobbes was the first to deduce rights and obligations from facts without putting anything fanciful in the facts.

Of course, Hobbes' own political convictions led him to conclude that natural equality had to give way to a more authoritarian system, which citizens would be obliged to obey (unless, as David Dyzenhaus reminds us, the sovereign threatened one's life and violated the social contract). It is just these movements, from defending staunch natural equality to upholding more hierarchical visions, that so grasped Macpherson's attention.

Macpherson had a great deal of respect for this liberal "revolution" in political thought; both for its realistic denunciation of "fanciful" notions of hierarchy that postulated some naked apes were mysteriously to others, and for its moral egalitarianism. The key question of the book therefore became how a doctrine as foundationally egalitarian and liberalism became aligned with the dramatic inequalities of wealth and power emblematic of capitalism.

Possessive individualism and neoliberalism

This is where Macpherson's core idea of "possessive individualism" arrived. He was especially fascinated by Locke's claims about how the basic equality of human beings linked with a distinctively bourgeois conception of property. They projected back onto the state of nature principles and contexts which were specific to the natal capitalism emerging in seventeenth-century England. Here is where classical liberal thought shifted from realistic materialism stressing our biological similarities and drawing plausible notions of equality therein to more ideological forms of mythmaking. The individual in the state of nature was conceived not just as a moral equal to all her fellows but as owning her body and her labour capacity. As Macpherson observed in *Possessive Individualism*:

[The present study] suggests that the difficulties of modern liberal-democratic theory lie deeper than had been thought, that the original seventeenth-century individualism contained the central difficulty, which lay in its possessive quality. Its possessive quality is found in its conception of the individual as essentially the proprietor of his own person or capacities, owing nothing to society for them. The individual was seen neither as a moral whole, nor as part of a larger social whole, but as an owner of himself. The relation of ownership, having become for more and more men the critically important relation determining their actual freedom and actual prospect of realizing their full potentialities, was read back into the nature of the individual. The individual, it was thought, is free inasmuch as he is proprietor of his person and capacities. The human essence is freedom from dependence on the wills of others, and freedom is a function of possession. Society becomes a lot of free equal individuals related to each other as proprietors of their own capacities and of what they have acquired by their exercise. Society consists of relations of exchange between proprietors. Political society becomes a calculated device for the protection of this property and for the maintenance of an orderly relation of exchange.

Then, though mixing her labour with the matter of the universe, she came to own external forms of property, which could not be expropriated without violating natural rights. As Locke put it in the *Second Treatise of Government*:

God, who hath given the world to men in common, hath also given them reason to make use of it to the best advantage of life, and convenience... Though the earth, and all inferior creatures, be common to all men, yet every man has a property in his own person: this no body has any right to but himself. The labour of his body, and the work of his hands, we may say, are properly his. Whatsoever then he removes out of the state that nature hath provided, and left it in, he hath mixed his labour with, and joined to it something that is his own, and thereby makes it his property. It being by him removed from the common state nature hath placed it in, it hath by this labour something annexed to it, that excludes the common right of other men: for this labour being the unquestionable property of the labourer, no man but he can have a right to what that is once joined to, at least where there is enough, and as good, left in common for others.

These rights to the fruit of one's labour were held to be natural and inviolable. Unless, and this is key, an individual chose to alienate her rights to the fruit her labour by offering it to another as part of a contract. On a vulgar Lockean reading this would become more likely as the originally free land of the earth became private property, depriving many of the opportunity to obtain agrarian independence through their efforts. Locke himself seemed aware of this and insisted that one could obtain natural rights to property, but only by leaving "as much, and as good" in common for others.

Many later classical liberals would not be so generous in their sensitivity to egalitarian demands and the need to inoculate people against the dangers of deprivation. Authors like Ludwig von Mises even chastised authors like Locke and the "liberals of the eighteenth century" for their "ill founded...assertion of the alleged equality of all members of the human race." On this telling, the market enabled superior persons to strike it rich and rise up the social hierarchy, and there could be very few, if any, legitimate arguments for redistributing their status or wealth which didn't lead to authoritarianism.

Through these modes of reasoning, early classical liberals were able to justify a system of thought that began with a commitment to radical equality and ownership of one's labour before ending with a defence of wage labour where the wealthy could reap enormous rewards by living off the contracted labour of others. Aligned with this was a realization on the part of classical liberals that such a system might lead to widespread inequality and anger. This is part of the reason the state became necessary to protect property rights and the inequities which resulted from them. In one of his more stinging passages, Macpherson notes the irony of an *individualist* doctrine like classical liberalism calling for a state to enforce stratified property rights over and against the potential wishes of the mass of people.

The notion that individualism and "collectivism" are the opposite ends of a scale along which states and theories of the state can be arranged, regardless of the stage of social development in which they appear, is superficial and misleading. Locke's individualism, that of an emerging capitalist society, does not exclude but on the contrary demands the supremacy of the state over the individual. It is not a question of the more thorough-going the individualism, the less collectivism; rather, the more thorough-going the individualism, the more complete the collectivism.

This critique of classical liberal thinking, beginning from radical equality and individualism and ending in a kind of despotic collectivism managed in the interest of property owners, is hardly a fable. It is emblematic of the neoliberal era in which we live. As Frank Cunnigham points out in *The Political Thought of C.B. Macpherson,* neoliberalism is a distinctly vicious form of possessive individualism defined by offering "justifications for the subordination of societies to the mandates of an economic market."

This subordination was quite complete by the 2010s. As social scientists have repeatedly shown neoliberal states have been characterized by plutocratic rule, where ordinary citizens have little influence on laws and policies, even in nominally democratic states. The elites adopted many of the core tenets of possessive individualism by conceiving the market as a sorting mechanism in which each person has a chance to deploy their capacity to labor to advance themselves. The fact that it is a wildly unequal chance was either ignored or naturalized as a necessary feature of market society. What emerged, as Michael Sandel reminds us, was a ruling elite which for the first time in history felt it entirely merited its affluence and consequently owed nothing to those at the bottom. Inversely, the mass of people left behind by neoliberalism have been characterized as lazy failures who deserve their lot. It should be no surprise that a figure like Trump, dividing the world into winners and losers, should emerge from such an uninspiring nullity which fantasized that it was the apex of human accomplishment.

Retrieving the best in liberalism

What made Macpherson's Left critique of the liberal tradition distinctive was that he never abandoned hope that one could retrieve its better and more human nature. As William Leiss putt it in *C.B. Macpherson: Dilemmas of Liberalism and Socialism,* the mature Macpherson always emphasized the many "*virtues of the liberal-democratic tradition, and especially the great importance of the commitment to civil liberties within it...*" Much of his mature work was centered around what Macpherson referred to as "retrieval" in his classic collection *Democratic Theory.* The goal was to "retrieve" the egalitarian and humanist core of liberalism that had fired the imagination of millions through a careful analysis of subsumed but not yet lost modes of thinking within the tradition.

Core to this was Macpherson's claim that a possessive individualist anthropology and attendant acquisitive ethic weren't ubiquitous across the liberal tradition. Possessive individualists saw man as an "infinite appropriator" concerned to acquire as much as possible within circumscribed rules in order to gratify his appetites. But by the nineteenth century, Macpherson thought many liberals came to reject this notion as both too crude and too anti-egalitarian. Chief among them was the quintessential liberal (and socialist) John Stuart Mill, whom in *The Rise and Fall of Economic Justice and Other Essays* Macpherson describes as enacting a "watershed" transition in liberal thought. This is because Mill was "concerned to rescue human values from their then subordination to the market." The Millsean state was not intended to "facilitate an endless increase in the production of wealth but to fashion a society with higher ends. [Mill] was thus, we might say, opposed in principle to the economic penetration of political theory."

Here we need to emphasize the importance of this transition more forcefully than Macpherson himself, who acknowledged the accomplishment of Left-liberals like Mill but was rarely able to express much more than ambivalence about it. Mill rejected possessive individualism and the acquisitive ethic characteristic of classical liberals, while taking up the tradition's defense of liberty, equality, and solidarity more forcefully than before. Mill acknowledged that our individuality was often the fruit of our interactions with other people, and in *Socialism* noted how capitalism very often inhibited its full realization. It articulated a bad principle of "individualism" as possessive and acquisitive, leading to competition, each one for himself and against all the rest. It is grounded in opposition of interests, not harmony of interests, and under it every one is required to find his place by a struggle, by pushing others back or being pushed back by them. Socialists consider this system of private war (as it may be termed) between every one and every one especially fatal from an economic as well as a moral point of view. Morally considered, its evils are obvious. It is the parent of envy, hatred, and all uncharitableness; it makes every one the natural enemy of all others who cross his path.

By contrast, following Macpherson, we can recognize how Mill's liberal socialism emphasized that our individualism could only flourish in the right social settings, where the human capacities of all could be developed thoroughly. Macpherson was highly attracted to this ideal. In *The Life and Times of Liberal Democracy* he described it as a liberal "developmental" democracy, which recognized that the:

> moral vision of the possibility of the improvement of mankind, an of a free and equal society [is] not yet achieved. A democratic political system is valued as a means to that improvement — a necessary though not a sufficient means; and a democratic society is seen as both a result of that improvement and a means to further improvement. The improvement that is expected is an increase in the amount of self-development of all the members of the society, or in John Stuart Mill's phrase the "advancement of community…in intellect, in virtue, and in practical activity and efficiency."

This Millsean ideal of a liberal socialist developmental democracy, or something rather like it, is an inspiring one. It takes more seriously than possessive individualist neoliberalism the importance of liberty and equality for all, and connects it to a developmental ethic insisting we allow each person a more robust opportunity to lead a good life through the development of their human capacities. This developmental ethic was also defended as an "Aristotelean principle" by Rawls in *A Theory of Justice.* Rawls notes that, "other things being equal, human beings enjoy the exercise of their realized capacities (their innate or trained abilities), and this enjoyment increases the more the capacity is realized, or the greater its complexity." Unfortunately, under current conditions, the least well-off will struggle to develop their "realized capacities" and employ them in truly satisfying enterprises. Indeed, millions in rich states will wind up working for Jeff Bezos and at best aspire to realize their capacity to pee freely whenever they wish.

If liberals are going to retain or regain the trust of those disappointed in its promises we need to offer much more than a replay of possessive individualism and its enormous and vapid range of failures. Macpherson was right to warn twentieth-century liberals that if they didn't live up to the best in their tradition, they would live down to the worst and see it end. Liberals in the twenty-first century would be wise to heed his lesson and do better than our predecessors.

ON RACIAL AND RADICAL LIBERALISMS[1]

Debates about race and the legacy of racism have long dominated American politics. This spans the political spectrum, from the recent feverish efforts of conservatives to detect critical race theory everywhere to the Left-liberal characterization of Trumpism as a fundamentally racist and xenophobic movement. This would no doubt come as a surprise to those who optimistically — and often self-servingly — hoped that the passage of civil rights legislation in the 1960s would bury these controversies once and for all without fundamentally challenging meritocratic mythologies to which many seem addicted.

A lot of the controversy turns on the accusation that liberalism is itself implicated in the history of racist oppression. This is a damning criticism of a political tradition that presents itself as always occupying the right side of history, at least in terms of promoting tolerance and inclusion. Responsible liberals will admit that plenty of their predecessors held racist views, and even that many early liberal societies propagated racist policies and propaganda. But defenders of liberalism will claim that this is largely circumstantial, and doesn't weigh heavily on the largely progressive accomplishments of the liberal tradition.

---

1   Reprinted from *Liberal Currents*.

In other words racism is an epiphenomenal bug in the liberal tradition which has largely been eradicated. This leaves the hard core of liberalism and liberal institutions largely untouched and renders further reforms unnecessary, even dangerous. To expunge the last vestiges of racism in contemporary society, we need only remove some lingering racist policies and condemn individual instances of racism where they pop up. Commentators in this vein typically argue that the ongoing fixation on race has had a corrosive effect on politics. This can come even from those who acknowledge that the history of racism and other forms of discrimination does have a lingering impact on people's life prospects, such as the right-wing liberal George Will. He articulates his frustration in a recent book, *The Conservative Sensibility.*

> The premise of [progressivism] is that identities, and rights, should derive from group membership, and special rights are owed to grievance groups composed of America's myriad and ever-multiplying victims. A corollary of this theory is "categorical representation," the idea that the interests of particular groups can be understood and articulated only by members of those groups... Progressives steeped in identity politics are not convinced that people can be readily reached by reason. Rather, progressives regard people as defined by, and enclosed in, their race, ethnicity, class, or gender. This leads to a contraction of the ambit of the democratic politics of persuasion. The vacated social space is filled by the brokering of identity-group interests in the name of a spurious equality of opportunity. The creation of "minority-majority" congressional districts expresses the ideology of identity politics: You are whatever your racial or ethnic group is.

The raw problem for right-wing liberals like Will is that race still matters an awful lot for life outcomes, whether we are talking about rates of criminalization and incarceration or the staggering disparities in family wealth between groups. Not to mention bigger historical questions about the legitimacy of states and systems of law built by imperialists and colonizers. This has led critics to argue that the history of liberalism can't be so easily disentangled from issues of race or racism, and that efforts to avoid this problem invariably legitimate injustices and disparities in the present. This reflects what the Marxist critic Domenico Losurdo calls the "hermeneutics of innocence," interpreting major authors and traditions so as to expunge their ugliest views and insulate their overall perspective from the most fundamental criticisms.

Charles Mills's critique of racial liberalism

One of the most probing critiques in this vein was pioneered by the late Jamaican-American philosopher Charles Mills. First presented in his book *The Racial Contract*, and culminating in *Black Rights/White Wrongs: The Critique of Racial Liberalism*, Mills argues that it is historically inaccurate to argue racism was a minor or incidental feature of liberalism. In Mills's view of liberalism, the "key terms have been written by race, and the discursive logic shaped accordingly." For Mills, European and American liberal theorists undoubtedly made important arguments for certain kinds of emancipatory politics, but they were nevertheless committed to "establishing and maintaining imperial and colonial rule abroad, and nonwhite racial subordination at home." If true, this obviously makes it far more challenging to exorcise the history of racism from liberal societies, since it is not extraneous but built into the very core of liberal philosophy and practices.

Despite his fierce criticisms, Mills argues that liberalism isn't beyond redemption, since many of its core moral claims can be extricated from the "contingent" reality of classical liberals' support for white supremacy. Mills acknowledges some major liberal thinkers deserve more blame for overtly supporting racial oppression than others. But even the better liberals often relegate commentary on race to a few lamentations before moving on to their central raceless ideal theory. Carrying out a liberal redemptive project will require that contemporary liberals adopt a "tough love" approach to the tradition and quit downplaying the centrality of race and racism in theory and practice.

Racial liberals: John Locke

An example of the centrality of racism to the liberal tradition can be seen in the work of John Locke. Often held up to be the founder of classical liberalism, Locke is perhaps most famous for his arguments about natural rights to life, liberty and property, and his claims about a social contract by the people to establish representative government. Locke notably influenced the American founders, and he is often taken to be a revolutionary defender of equality and liberty. Mills points out that this rosy interpretation of Locke ignores that he not only invested in African slavery but justified "aboriginal expropriation." This wasn't incidental bigotry but central to his entire philosophy. In the *Second Treatise of Government,* Locke argues that in the beginning God had

> given the world to men in common, hath also given them reason to make use of it to the best advantage of life, and convenience. The earth, and all that is therein, is given to men for the support and comfort of their being. And tho' all the fruits it naturally produces, and beasts it feeds, belong

to mankind in common, as they are produced by the spon-
taneous hand of nature; and no body has originally a private dominion, exclusive of the rest of mankind, in any of
them, as they are thus in their natural state: yet being given
for the use of men, there must of necessity be a means to
appropriate them some way or other, before they can be of
any use, or at all beneficial to any particular man. The fruit,
or venison, which nourishes the wild Indian, who knows
no enclosure, and is still a tenant in common, must be his,
and so his, i.e. a part of him, that another can no longer
have any right to it, before it can do him any good for the
support of his life.

The reference to the "wild Indian" is important. Locke later
argues that while we all originally possessed the world in
common, it didn't stay that way. As one of the founders of
the political theory of "possessive individualism," Locke
argued that individuals gained rights to private property
through mixing their labor with the matter of the earth,
as through agriculture. An isolated piece of land that once
laid fallow becomes someone's possession, as do its fruits,
when he encloses and improves it to produce crops.

Locke goes on to argue that while the state is obligated
to respect natural rights to property flowing from labor,
no one possesses such rights in North America. This is
because, despite the presence of indigenous peoples, these
lands remain uncultivated and so are still the common
property of all. He asks "whether in the wild woods and
uncultivated waste of America, left to nature, without any
improvement, tillage or husbandry, a thousand acres yield
the needy and wretched inhabitants as many conveniences
of life, as ten acres of equally fertile land do in Devonshire,
where they are well cultivated?" The implication is that
privatizing the allegedly common space of North America
through transforming it into property along the European

model would ultimately make it more productive. It was part of a civilizing project.

Of course, the millions of original inhabitants living in North America may well have thought they had some entitlement to the land of their ancestors, whether they used it in a manner amenable to Locke or not. By denying them this entitlement, Locke provided ideological ammunition with which later liberals like Jefferson would justify colonial expansion westward, and when this was resisted by the inhabitants, call for a war of "extermination." Or as Ayn Rand would later put it with characteristic brutality: the aboriginals had "no right to a country merely because they were born here and then acted like savages... Since the Indians did not have the concept of property or property rights — they didn't have a settled society."

Racial liberals: Immanuel Kant

Another example that particularly stings for those of us with a deontological bent is Mills's foregrounding of Immanuel Kant's racism. Though Kant is often held up to be the exemplary philosopher of universal human dignity and freedom, Mills notes the tremendous theoretical energy Kant applied to his racist science and anthropology. Kant characterized "Negroes" as among the "lowest" forms of humanity, described the white race as possessing "all motivating forces and talents in itself," and infantilized Native Americans, who are described as incapable of "love, thus they are also not afraid. They hardly speak, do not caress each other, care about nothing and are lazy."

This was not merely incidental prejudice from Kant (who by most accounts rarely set foot outside of Konigsberg), easily set aside when dealing with his thought. Mills argues that Kant's racism tarnishes a significant part of his philosophy. While Kant does indeed argue that our status as transcendentally free and rational moral agents entitles us to be treated with dignity, he seems to have denied that non-whites were in fact free and rational moral agents in this transcendental sense. Due to their biological inferiority, they needn't be considered members of the human community in the same sense as white Europeans. If true, it would mean that any use of Kant's work needs to commit itself to some serious rethinking of its foundations. As Mills puts it:

> Instead of presenting that Kant was arguing for equal respect to be extended to everybody, we should be asking how Kant's theory needs to be rethought in light not merely of his own racism but of a modern world with a normative architecture based on racist Kant-like principles. How is "respect" to be cashed out, for example, for a population that has historically been seen as less than persons? Should it be reconceptualized with a supplementary group dimension, given that white supremacy has stigmatized entire races as less than worthy of respect, as appropriately to be "dissed?" What corrective measures would be required of the *Rechsstaat* to redress racial subordination?

This claim is considerably more controversial, and in my view unconvincing. While Kant undoubtedly held these opinions, the drift of his thinking near the end of his life and at his peak of theoretical maturity seemed to be toward greater egalitarianism. His transcendental argument about the *a priori* and universal structure of human consciousness can be criticized for its inattentiveness to the impact of external inputs, such as how language influences how we think. But it doesn't seem that anything fundamental in *The Critique of Pure Reason* turns on Kant's racism.

Even if it turned out that Kant's biological racism (and misogyny) did entail denying equal transcendental status to some, we needn't follow him in that. I am also less convinced that Kant's politics were as revanchist as Mills makes out. Commentators like Arthur Ripstein have given new life to the interpretation of Kant as a revolutionary critical thinker, and he undoubtedly became more critical of imperialism and colonialism. This would be more consistent with the thrust of Kant's philosophy, which even Mills sets out to salvage at the end of *Black Rights/White Wrongs*. Nevertheless, Mills's critique of Kant remains potent, and no one writing in his wake should be uncritical of the German philosopher's racial arguments or ignore the problems they pose for interpreting his philosophy as a whole.

Can liberalism still be radical?

The payoff of Mills's critiques is that by alerting us to liberalism's foundational failings on race he awakens us to how much more still needs to be done by liberals of good conscience. George Will and others may disparage the metaphor of the "race of life" often appealed to by critical race theorists like Kimberlé Crenshaw, suggesting we only look at overall improvements in life outcomes. After all, if the absolute positions of individuals within racialized groups are better now than in the 1960s, what else is that but improvement? And just so. But there is nothing irrational about acknowledging that improvements in the lives of racialized people are good, while recognizing they are far short of what is both achievable and fair.

If I pay John $80 to landscape my yard, and next week pay Jane $10 for the same task, there is nothing unusual in Jane recognizing her situation has improved while still thinking the disparity is grossly unfair. Calling for fairness isn't resentment. It is a demand for a kind of justice. So long as we live in a competitive society where some people gain more than others, the metaphor of a race of life seems appropriate. As does Crenshaw's argument that some of us are given premium training while others are forced to run from 400 yards back with weights in their shoes, all while still describing our society as an equal meritocracy.

Nevertheless, liberalism can be saved from this racist legacy, even if doing so will entail more than just dropping some overtly bigoted policies and language. At the end of his life, Mills argued for a "black radical liberalism" that kept what was most egalitarian and emancipatory in the tradition, but shifted matters of racial injustice and disparities in power from the periphery to center focus. I would argue that we need many radical liberalisms to address these and other problems. As Mills himself shows, the liberal tradition is a broad family which can include a wide variety of different perspectives on issues like equality and racial justice. A radical and anti-racist liberalism would emphasize the core egalitarian values of liberalism, but situate them in a more muscular critique of contemporary (neo)liberal society as it exists now. It would pay special attention to the particular forms that domination and marginalization have taken — avoiding too much abstraction — and develop specifically liberal responses. In other words it would mean stepping away from what Mills calls purely "ideal" theory and engaging in the messy power dynamics that so define our lived reality.

An anti-racist radical liberalism

Ironically Mills leans heavily on Kant as a potential foundation for black radical liberalism, along with Karl Marx and W.E.B. Du Bois. This was despite his critique of Kant's racism, and because Kant was the "most important theorist of the dominant variety of contemporary liberalism, 'deontological' liberalism." In particular, Kant's stress on the innate dignity of persons needs to be categorically extended to people of color. But for Mills, taking this seriously requires more than formalistic declarations of personhood. There needs to be a concerted effort to "correct for [the] past history" of racial discrimination, which would require very dramatic changes indeed.

Here Mills turns to Rawls's contractarianism, but argues that we need to reconceive the project as "tearing up the bad contract that has created the world we live in" by allowing reasoners to take into account the history of racism in the United States and elsewhere rather than abstracting away such details as in Rawls's original "veil of ignorance." This would allow them to deliberate on how best to rectify the injustices that have resulted from this history. Sadly, Mills passed away before his ideas went much beyond a preliminary sketch, which means it is incumbent on us to try to build upon his still germinating insights. I would argue that the form of liberalism best suited to realizing Mills's aspirations would be a form of liberal socialism that addresses racial oppression alongside class oppression, rather than as a side issue. In what follows I'll offer further ways of rethinking the liberal tradition which might be useful to that effect.

The first would be to follow Mills in reconfiguring Rawls for more radical purposes. This would be consistent with Rawls's own thinking, which by the time of *Justice as Fairness: A Restatement* had already moved in a more progressive direction. By the 2000s, Rawls was losing confidence that the United States could still be characterized as a reasonably just society, or that the moderate welfarism people gleaned from *Theory of Justice* could be sufficient. Instead he agitated directly for a kind of "property owning democracy" or "liberal socialism." One of the more intriguing arguments he raised for this position was that a failure to establish a high level of economic well being for the least well-off didn't just impact their quality of life materially; it depleted the value of other liberties, particularly political liberties. By allowing wealth and power to concentrate in the hands of a plutocratic elite, the political liberties we're nominally supposed to enjoy equally become far more valuable to the few than the many. This would have been no surprise to theorists like Marx; empirical researchers like Martin Gilens have highlighted how the rich enjoy vastly more political influence than the average American citizen.

The importance of equal political liberties for all is especially germane when even today racism is connected with *de jure* or *de facto* disenfranchisement. For over a century, black Americans were denied even basic rights, and even after the American Civil war a variety of insidious mechanisms were used to disenfranchise newly freed slaves and re-entrench white supremacy. Sadly, this is not mere history, as conservative groups employ everything from gerrymandering to felony disenfranchisement to marginalize black voices. These efforts are deeply unjust from a Rawlsian standpoint, since they either outright deprive people of even basic political liberties or ensure that these are less valuable than those enjoyed by white elites.

In her book *The Tyranny of the Majority: Fundamental Freedoms in Representative Democracy,* the late Lani Guinier suggested replacing the racially biased democratic system with one that is "is procedurally fair to the extent that it gives each participant an equal opportunity to influence [democratic] outcomes." This would involve regulating and ideally eliminating gerrymandering by race, eliminating the more anti-majoritarian features of the US electoral system, and of course eliminating restrictions on voting rights which disproportionately impact the racially marginalized. This is absolutely the right idea, and suggests the deep affinity radical liberalism would need to have with the democratization of society. I would add that this approach would mean eradicating ongoing measures that discriminate *de jure* or *de facto* by race, curbing the influence of money in politics and emphasizing a newly democratic and egalitarian culture. This would help answer a substantial part of Mills's challenge that liberal institutions are frequently unresponsive to racial issues because there is a lack of accountability built into them. By ensuring all have equal opportunities to influence democratic outcomes, marginalized groups would form a more substantial power block to which representatives would have to be accountable.

One of the reasons democracy is so important to radical liberalism is because it is one of the ways we can construct a shared world together on the basis of mutual respect and co-operation. This has a deep affinity with economic issues. As Cornel West observed in his classic *Race Matters*: "We must focus our attention on the public square — the common good that undergirds our national and global destinies. The vitality of any public square depends on how much we care about the quality of our lives together." But the past decades have seen the stagnation or rollback of redistributive efforts and workers' movements that contributed to the provision of public goods and the ensuring of wellbeing for all. This rollback has had a negative impact on many of us, but as Kimberlé Crenshaw points out, it disproportionately affects racialized groups due to the vast disparities of wealth and opportunity caused by structural racism.

One way of responding to this from a radical liberal perspective would entail adopting a more egalitarian distributive principle which requires us to foreground the needs of the least well-off. Rawls "difference principle" — which only allows inequalities to the extent they benefit the least well-off — would be a good candidate, particularly in its later liberal socialist formulations. But we would need to sharpen its critical edges. Rawls argues that the difference principle would be chosen for two reasons. Firstly, self-interested reasoners behind a veil of ignorance would choose it as the right principle for society since they would not want to risk being severely disadvantaged in a highly unequal economy. Mills proposes to allow those behind the veil to perceive the effects of structural racism, as this is part of the "basic structure" of society. Rawlsian reasoners would thus also justify more tailored applications of the difference principle to address the negative impacts of racial inequality they are aware of.

Rawls's second justification for the difference principle is that most of the reasons for inequalities in society are "morally arbitrary." People wind up where they are because of a combination of fortune, social circumstance, and the design of institutions. This obviously cuts deeply against both traditional conservative and meritocratic arguments that defend hierarchy on the basis that the more deserving deserve more. Yet Rawls's arguments about moral arbitrariness, like Kant's own deontological ruminations, are highly formalized and technical. They rightly hold that people's position in society has little to do with individual will, choice, or inherent qualities. But they spare little time considering how social (e.g., racial) structures can also be determinative. This risks renaturalizing the roots of inequality even if it provides refined tools to criticize and repair its consequences. In the face of Rawls's arguments about moral arbitrariness, we need to recognize that many of the material inequalities that emerge are not just arbitrary but the result of structural disparities a just society would seek to rectify. This means that efforts to care for the less well-off can't involve only redistributing resources downward, but must also eliminate persistent structural barriers to racial equality.

Following Du Bois, one obvious example — of special relevance now — would be ending the vast disparities in the quality of early education. This is in no small part due to a bizarre system which allows wealthy families to spend more on educating children in their districts while allocating little if anything to others. This has enabled the persistence of educational disparities which map onto racial inequality, and it incentivizes the wealthy to ignore what goes on in schools where they have no stake. Equal education for all is a sensible measure which would improve outcomes by investing everyone in the quality of each child's development.

Conclusion

An anti-racist radical liberalism may seem like an oxymoron to those who associate the tradition with racism, imperialism, and xenophobia. Mills shows us that even the greatest liberal thinkers were infatuated with everything from race science to mythologies of imperial grandeur. All those sides to the liberal tradition are still with us, and liberals are often tempted by more overtly right-wing arguments that the best society is one where the recognizably "superior" rule. While overt appeals to racial superiority are less common than a generation ago, they have hardly disappeared and undoubtedly achieved a major comeback circa Trumpist anxieties about immigration and the changing complexion of the American public. Trump himself tied these racial anxieties to a neoliberal ethic of meritocracy, presenting himself and his followers as self-made men victimized by envious "losers." Underpinning this was a great deal of ressentiment at seeing one's cherished privileges democratized, undermining the status and auspicion associated with them.

But there is another side to the liberal tradition that can be radicalized for the purposes of achieving justice for the racially oppressed in particular. This would require dropping the more abstract formalism of liberalism for a sensitivity to material and historical circumstance that even the most progressive liberal theorists have often lacked. Yet this needn't be an entirely one-sided exchange. Mills was very critical of liberalism, but in the end he identified with the tradition. Liberalism's commitment to freedom and equality for all remains profoundly attractive, however imperfectly that commitment has been realized. One of the great weaknesses in the purely "critical" disciplines which have emerged, and which fixate on "trashing" at all costs, is precisely that they refrain from offering realistic alternatives to the neoliberal and racially stratified status quo. This contributes to what Cornel West rightly describes as the "nihilism" emblematic of the era: the belief that injustice is so entrenched and powerful that it can at best be recognized but never overcome.

Rather than giving into these impulses, we should see the liberal tradition as flawed but not beyond redemption. The liberal socialist and radical liberal tradition of Mill, Rawls, Mouffe and Mills offers a clear vision for how to dramatically reform society while retaining what is best within it. Those of us who want to save the best sides of liberalism need to continue Mills's decoupling of theory and practice from its racial and discriminatory baggage, while showing how a more refined liberal approach can speak to our yearning for justice in the twenty-first century.

THE SOCIALIST POLITICS AND THEOLOGY OF PAUL TILLICH[1]

The German theologian Paul Tillich (1886–1965) is renowned today for his powerful synthesis of Christian theology and existentialism. He released an acclaimed series of short books written during the 1950s, including the evocative titles *The Courage to Be* and *Dynamics of Faith*. These texts laid out Tillich's dynamic theology with a rare combination of economy and mystery, memorably describing "faith as a state of being ultimately concerned" and declaring that "courage can show us what Being truly is." Later, he authored an epic three-volume *Systematic Theology*, which dove deep into the murk of existentialist philosophy, famously arguing that God constitutes the ultimate "ground of Being" implied in humanity's search for self-transcendence.

While Tillich has become a veritable giant within contemporary theology, many are not familiar with his lifelong commitment to socialism, in both theory and practice. Tillich was active in Germany's religious socialism movement and became deeply conversant with Marxist theory and politics. Notably, he authored a lesser-known book, *The*

---

1   Reprinted from *Jacobin*.

Socialist Decision, in which he argued for the necessity of socialism in the twentieth century — and which he deemed his best work.

Socialism was no mere academic matter for Tillich. He served as a chaplain during World War I, an experience that brought him face-to-face with the catastrophes of capitalism and militarism, as well as the political anemia of the Christian churches. He returned home to his native Germany, which was quickly turned upside down by the 1918 November Revolution. Kaiser Wilhelm II's empire gave way to the cultural roller coaster of the Weimar Republic, and Tillich and his second wife, Hannah Werner-Gottschow, embraced its social liberalism and experimentalism. They lived in an open marriage and frequented the avant-garde venues and social circles of the time.

Soon after the war's conclusion, Tillich began to participate in working groups and intellectual circles with other religious socialists. In an early pamphlet coauthored in 1919, he urged "representatives of Christianity and the church who stand on socialist soil to enter into the socialist movement in order to pave the way for a future union of Christianity and the socialist social order."

Then, in 1932, came his book *The Socialist Decision*, written as the Nazis transitioned from a threatening political movement to a lethal political dictatorship. Tillich's politics had already made him a liability for the Nazi Party, and the book was immediately censored. He was allegedly offered a prestigious academic position on the condition that he repudiate the book and its criticisms of the new regime. Tillich laughed and was swiftly exiled to the United States, where he and Hannah lived out the remainder of their days.

The Perils of Political Romanticism

Though nearly all initial copies of *The Socialist Decision* were destroyed by the Nazis and the fires of war, a few remained in circulation among Tillich's confidantes. Nearly forty years later, it was translated into English. *The Socialist Decision* is an underappreciated and highly unique contribution to the tradition of religious socialism. In addition to its theological insight, it exhibits great imagination and political sensitivity in dealing with the perils and contradictions of Tillich's time. As waves of right-wing populism and illiberal movements crash against the institutions of democracy in the twenty-first century, *The Socialist Decision* deserves to be revisited and applied to our political moment.

One of the main targets of Tillich's book is political romanticism, which he defines as a nostalgic attachment to a "myth of origin [that] envisions the beginnings of humankind in elemental, superhuman figures of various kinds." This myth of the origin is one of the great "roots of political thought" and is the basis for all "conservative and romantic thought in politics." Tillich discerned three basic origin myths that animate romantic politics: soil, blood, and social group.

These myths of origin help to sanction the present in two primary ways. First, they idealize a paternalistic past in order to "hold consciousness fast, not allowing it to escape from their dominion." Second, they resist the demands of justice by freezing historical time into a recurring cycle of rise and fall. As Tillich writes, "The origin embodies the law of cyclical motion: whatever proceeds from it must return to it. Wherever the origin is in control, nothing new can happen."

Myths of origin take on a special role in the wake of capitalism and liberalism, forming a bulwark against modern ideas of individualism, egalitarianism, and the rational improvement of society. Such myths imagine a transhistorical founding of the people or state — one beyond questions of legitimacy and justice — that establishes strict hierarchies and naturalizes the existence of social classes. This mythical order depends on an elite few with elevated status and powers of rule over the underclasses; when the dominated classes attempt to deviate from this order, inevitable chaos and ruin follows.

Though Tillich was concerned mainly with the rise of Nazism, his analysis is highly applicable to twenty-first-century conservatism. Origin myths are highly adaptable to different political and social circumstances, and are easily wielded by both religious and secular interests. For instance, many conservative Christians interpret human history through a pseudo-Augustinian lens of endless decline and fall. In effect, "nothing new can happen": it is our fate to endlessly repeat the Edenic fall from grace, as virtuous religious societies emerge, fall into sinful permissiveness and decadence, and collapse in ruin.

Tillich's metaphors of soil and social group, which emphasize a primal rootedness and connection, are clearly deployed by nationalists to instill a sense of organic belonging and imagined community. The culturally and racially homogenous nation is contrasted with a decrepit one, polluted by unrestrained multiculturalism and the presence of foreign aliens — those who are not "native" to the soil and become parasites on national culture and institutions.

The most insidious myth of origin, according to Tillich, is the "animal form of origin" or "origin of blood." This myth embraces violent hierarchy and racial superiority, imagining a clash with other "animal powers in a process of selection through struggle and breeding." Rather than describing the long fall in terms of grace and sin, or vibrant national culture and decadent decay, it invokes the starkly racial crises of genetic pollution and demographic decline. Today, the Right increasingly relies on these tropes: right-wing figures like Charles Murray and Andrew Sullivan have re-popularized notions of "race science,"[2] while Tucker Carlson breathlessly warns five million viewers about the impending "great replacement" of white voters.[3]

The Conservative Uses of Origin Myths

Despite the varied and sometimes contradictory uses of these myths by the contemporary right, they all serve to rationalize a nostalgic attachment to a gloriously idealized past. Because the bogeymen of "liberalism," democracy," and/or "social justice" have severed society from its primordial origin, the present can be recast as merely a hollow shell. The modern revolt against political and social hierarchies have handed illegitimate power to the unworthy, the immoral, and the outsider — a power they cannot capably exercise. And so, paradoxically, the conservative must *fight* to bring the past into the present. As Corey Robin memorably notes, "Conservatism is about power besieged and power protected. It is an activist doctrine for an activist time."[4]

---

2   Gavin Evans, "The unwelcome revival of 'race science," *The Guardian*, March 2018: https://www.theguardian.com/news/2018/mar/02/the-unwelcome-revival-of-race-science

3   Johnathan Chait, "Tucker Carlson Endorses White Supremacist by Name," *NY Mag*, April 2021: https://nymag.com/intelligencer/2021/04/tucker-carlson-great-replacement-white-supremacist-immigration-fox-news-racism.html

4   Corey Robin, *The Reactionary Mind*, Oxford, 2017.

This point is very important, as liberals and Leftists often mistakenly assume that conservatism is primarily about the defense of the past. But in moments like Tillich's, when liberal institutions are vulnerable and social movements threaten to upset the status quo, the reactionary response must be equally activist. In pivotal political moments, the conservative cannot be a crotchety defender of the status quo, since it has become clear that cannot halt the underclasses' forward movement. Instead, conservatives must continually develop creative new forms of power to halt the decay of modernity and democracy — often by more effectively wielding the technological power and innovation that exploded in the modern era.

This paradoxical need to establish new forms of power by appealing to a romantic past easily leads to intense competition between conservative factions — both in Tillich's time and ours. Tillich captures this conflict by distinguishing between "conservative" and "revolutionary" romanticism. Conservative romanticism "defend[s] the spiritual and social residues of the bond of origin against the autonomous system, and whenever possible [seeks] to restore past forms." This kind of romanticism has animated much of modern conservatism, which usually tries to restore traditional forms of elite society by rolling back reforms, defending free markets, and neutralizing radical movements.

In an American context, the "fusionist" project of combining traditionalist conservatism with *laissez-faire* economics is emblematic of this tendency. But when liberalism threatens to be dragged to the left or traditional conservative elites falter, a more radical, "revolutionary" romanticism of the far right can emerge. Revolutionary romanticism "tries to gain a basis for new ties to the origin by a devastating attack on the rational system." It brooks few compromises with political institutions and attacks traditional elites for their inability to order and purify the national community. Where revolutionary romanticism gains ground, it launches its devastating attack against representative democracy, first by strategically collaborating with traditional elites and then violently crushing them and all political opposition. This is precisely what happened in 1930s Germany, when the youthful Nazis entered into an alliance with traditional conservative nationalists — only to brush them aside once they'd served their purpose.

Liberalism and Socialism: Friends or Foes?

Tillich's discussion of German liberalism and capitalism — both of which opened the door to Nazi reaction — is especially insightful for understanding our contemporary moment. Tillich was well aware that capitalism and liberalism arose as intertwined forces. Wielded by the capitalist class, liberalism was instrumental in severing society from traditional religious and communal bonds and introduced the world to the horrors of colonialism, imperialism, and slavery.

But the fact that liberalism and capitalism developed together did not lead Tillich to a dismissive critique of liberalism. Unlike some contemporary Christian theologians whose "anti-capitalism" involves categorically rejecting liberal modernity or rehabilitating preliberal political ideas, Tillich insisted on the necessity of liberalism for the socialist project. He praised liberalism's individualism, rationalism, and moral egalitarianism as indispensable for authentic democracy and socialism. As he put it, "Liberalism and democracy in fact belong very closely together. Each is at work within the other; and in spite of the sharpest tensions that may arise between them, they can never be separated."

However, Tillich was highly critical of the bourgeois capture of liberalism, which granted liberty and self-determination to the capitalist class and denied it to the masses. It was because the capitalist class had failed to "actualize the democratic demands of its own principle" that liberal political radicalism in the eighteenth and nineteenth century quickly gave way to abstract idealism. Tillich knew that liberalism could not be rolled back — this would be yet another romantic reaction. Instead, to truly realize the liberal promise, liberalism would have to be severed from the capitalist system that results in "total human objectification because of economic objectification."

In our time, liberalism and capitalism have also come under intense scrutiny from both the Right and the Left. One notable criticism comes from a growing number of right-wing, largely Catholic intellectuals who have called for an end to liberalism. This cadre of "postliberals" contends that political liberalism has given rise to a tyranny of secularism, individual autonomy, and transgressive identities. Because they believe that liberalism is inherently hostile toward traditional Christianity, postliberals have coalesced around a strong state (often aligning themselves with far-right politicians), fighting culture wars against "elites" and "wokeism" and rehabilitating a hegemonic "cultural Christianity."

Unlike "fusionist" conservatives, postliberals regularly criticize free markets for their role in maintaining liberalism. However, it is not *capitalism itself* that unsettles them but the pervasive market relations that threaten the "traditional" forms of social, sexual, and religious life they wish to maintain. Inevitably, their softball criticisms of consumerism, markets, and Wall Street take a back seat to more pressing anxieties — for instance, who gets to use which bathroom, or the scandal of drag queen library hours. The free market is bad not because it subjects us to social and political unfreedom but because it grants us *too much* freedom from our naturally "given" roles.

Though written nearly one hundred years ago, Tillich presciently grasped how these social conservative revolts against market tyranny play a role in the reproduction of capitalism:

> The apocalyptic pronouncements of doom which the intellectual groups of political romanticism direct at industrial society do not hinder the bearers of capitalistic power from using the new, supposedly anticapitalistic forms of social reconstruction to secure their own class dominance.

Tillich also anticipated the political vision entailed in postliberalism: a combination of authoritarian capitalism and nationalism. Stark market inequalities will be maintained alongside a state that advances illiberal social policies and suppresses progressive movements — all in the name of preserving a unitary national identity. As Tillich put it, "The bourgeoisie, with the help of the idea of the nation, succeeds in overcoming its political opponents at home, in enlisting in its service the pre-bourgeois forces that are still bound to the origin."

By contrast, Tillich offers a far more progressive account of Christianity that contains sharper anti-capitalist resources for the Left. Unlike today's postliberals, who want to suppress liberalism — and the marginalized subjects who have laid claim to liberalism's promises — Tillich knew that Christians must protect and *radicalize* the liberal legacy by deciding for socialism. He described this as the primary "internal conflict of socialism" rooted in the "internal conflict of the proletariat situation." For Tillich, the true realization of universal equality and freedom could only be attained in a courageous decision for a liberal, democratic socialism.

This would require a decisive break from myths of origin, and their pessimistic politics of grandiosity and dominance, as well as a commitment to a more human future beyond capitalism. As Tillich put it, "The breaking of the myth of origin by the unconditional demand is the roots [sic] of liberal, democratic, and socialist thought in politics." How this could be achieved in theory, let alone in practice, is the immense task that fell to socialists then — and now.

What Comes After a Failed Revolution?

One complicating issue for German socialism in the early twentieth century was its understanding of Marxism. Tillich adopted a nuanced, balanced approach to Karl Marx in *The Socialist Decision*, neither praising him as a biblical seer nor dismissing him for his "materialism" or "economism," as Christian theologians often do. Tillich found a great deal of moral value in the young Marx's critique of capitalist alienation, and extolled Marx's mature theory of historical materialism. But he was staunchly critical of "dogmatic" Marxists in Germany, who claimed to have discovered in *Capital* a lithomantic crystal that foretold an inevitable socialist future.

Tillich noted that belief an inexorable socialist victory became a lethal hallucinogen to many movements, as they vested their hopes in calculating the moment of crisis and revolution. As these confident hopes failed to materialize, a morbid sense of disappointment set in.

The belief that history moved irresistibly toward socialism contributed to a tendency among German Marxists to become detached from a materialist praxis bent on changing the world. Instead of waging a relentless struggle to obtain power and enact socialist reforms, too many radicals gave into theorizing ever more elaborate predictive models of how capitalism would collapse under the weight of its own contradictions. In a grim turn, heated Marxist debates about forming a united front with "reformist" social democrats against fascism resulted in a Nazi waltz to victory. Marxist theory had dictated that fascism was little more capitalism's dying gasp; instead, the Nazis marched social democrats and communists into the concentration camps.

There is another contemporary lesson to be drawn from Tillich's analysis of German Marxism. Since the vulgar Marxist belief in the inevitability of revolution sputtered and then died, the contemporary Left has fractured, and now spends a great deal of time mincing minute differences between social democrats, radicals, Left-liberals, communists, Marxists — often in a needlessly puritanical fashion.

While conservatives happily seize on this (disproportionately online) phenomenon as proof of Leftist intolerance, I hold a different view. As Ben Burgis and Natalie Wynn of *Contrapoints* have pointed out, much of this behavior is rooted in melancholia. Deflated by a sense of political impotence in the face of neoliberalism, Leftists increasingly turn to aesthetics, performance, and the cultivation of personal political brands.

Purity of spirit and staking out the most radical positions easily takes the place of the day-to-day work of engaging the masses and winning reforms that benefit working people. Small political achievements are deemed a distraction from revolutionary politics (both before and after they're won). Fellow Leftists who insist on more nuanced understandings of theory and practice are immediately told of the utter immutability of the systems of power and oppression we oppose. This dialectic of puritanical posturing and fatalistic resignation is one of the greatest obstacles to restoring hope among the Left that "we have it in our power to begin the world again." We should heed Tillich's corrective to Leftist melancholia, which invoked prophetic hope: "Socialism lifts up the symbol of expectation against the myth of origin and against the belief in harmony."

A Prophetic Demand, a Socialist Future

Tillich insisted on making a "decision" for socialism, and developing the courage to work toward achieving it. As the forces of conservative and revolutionary romanticism bear down on the twenty-first century, Christians and socialists cannot assume that the arc of history will bend toward emancipation without costly struggle and reactionary backlash. But this is no reason to retreat to a vulgar revolutionary optimism or melancholic puritanism. As Tillich observed, the superiority of the socialist principle is rooted in a "propheticism" that makes an "unconditional demand" on the present, rooted in a promised future. Tillich concluded in *The Socialist Decision*, "Only through expectation is human existence raised to the level of true humanity."

No one expressed this truly revolutionary expectation better than Tillich's greatest pupil, Martin Luther King, Jr., who deserves to have the final word on this point:

The question is not whether we will be extremists, but what kind of extremists we will be. Will we be extremists for hate or for love? Will we be extremists for the preservation of injustice or for the extension of justice? In that dramatic scene on Calvary's hill three men were crucified. We must never forget that all three were crucified for the same crime — the crime of extremism. Two were extremists for immorality, and thus fell below their environment. The other, Jesus Christ, was an extremist for love, truth and goodness, and thereby rose above his environment. Perhaps the South, the nation and the world are in dire need of creative extremists.

REVISITING TONY SMITH'S BEYOND LIBERAL EGALITARIANISM[1]

Recent decades have been kind to liberal and Marxist attempts at dialogue. But old animosities are like Henry Kissinger: they die slowly. Of course there are still considerable disagreements between liberals and Marxists on a wide variety of issues. This is especially true of classical liberals and libertarians, who still tend to treat Marxism as the mortal enemy of property rights and market freedoms.

Relations between Marxism and liberal egalitarianism are more complicated. Dating back to Thomas Paine and Mary Wollstonecraft, through the liberal socialism of John Stuart Mill and the more recent black radical liberalism of Charles Mills, there has long been a stream of liberal thought which takes seriously the inequalities and domination produced under conditions of economic inequality. These thinkers have regarded inequality and domination as problematic and potentially even incompatible with liberal justice. Indeed this anxiety is so deeply rooted in the liberal tradition that the two most important liberal philosophers of the nineteenth and twentieth century, John Stuart Mill

---

1   Reprinted from *Liberal Currents*.

and John Rawls, sympathized with socialism (Mill even overtly identified with socialism).

The Marxist side of the relationship is equally fraught. Marx himself is sometimes crudely painted, including by some vulgar Marxists, as a stridently anti-liberal thinker. For many, he exposed liberalism as nothing more than an ideological gloss intended to defend capitalist domination and private property (a caricature of liberalism some followers of Mises seem determined to live down to). In fact, Marx regarded liberalism and capitalism as together marking a clear advance on the old feudal system and the highest form of society yet achieved. Throughout his life, Marx supported a variety of liberal causes, from freedom of the press to universal suffrage, and he engaged respectfully with the writings of Smith, Ricardo, Hegel, and sometimes even Mill. Nevertheless, for a long time even the more sophisticated Marxist treatments of liberalism tended to see it as irrevocably flawed and fated to be superseded by a higher form of society. Even as perceptive a critic as Fredric Jameson, in *Valences of the Dialectic,* could describe any concession to liberal normative theory as a retreat for committed Marxists.

Tony Smith's defense of liberal egalitarianism

All this makes Tony Smith's seminal *Beyond Liberal Egalitarianism: Marx and Normative Social Theory in the Twenty-First Century* a delight. I would even call it the most important contribution to a dialogue between liberals and Marxists since C.B. MacPherson's analysis of possessive individualism. First published in 2017, Smith's book made waves among critical theorists for its highly sympathetic and textured criticisms of liberal egalitarianism. Unfortunately the book has yet to find a significant liberal audience. *Beyond Liberal Egalitarianism* sets the platinum standard for sophisticated and respectful dialogue between liberals and Marxists, without simplifying or avoiding hard truths.

Smith opens the book by chastising his fellow Marxists for their reductive and knee-jerk dismissals of liberal egalitarianism, which they characterize as little more than classical liberalism with a few welfarist flourishes. To these critics, liberal egalitarianism remains committed to the same hyper-individualistic and classist apologias for capitalist domination. Smith highlights three points where he thinks Marxists get liberal egalitarianism wrong.

The first is the Marxist claim that liberal egalitarians hold to the same atomistic individualism of Locke and Hobbes, wherein the "individual is conceptualized as the basic unit of the social world, and the pursuit of private self-interest is taken to be the basis of decision-making and action." Marxists maintain in contrast that the individual self is "inseparable from our place in a particular society at a particular time that has reached a particular historical level of material and cultural development and that reproduces itself through a particular set of social relations." Smith rightly points out that this stream of liberal thought is alive and well; especially within libertarianism.

But this objection falls flat against liberal egalitarians like Rawls or Martha Nussbaum, who are committed to "normative" but not "metaphysical" individualism. Liberal egalitarians think that "individuals are the ultimate units of moral concern" but can be very open to the observation that any individual is very much constituted through her broader set of social relations, and that having the right social relations is integral to her wellbeing. Indeed, Rawls held that the primary subject of justice was not the individual but the "basic structure of society" — a point he claimed was inspired by a reading of Hegel and Marx. The capabilities approach of Nussbaum and Amartya Sen carries forward Aristotle's observation that we are social creatures, and that the conditions of our individual flourishing are consequently also very much social and deeply interpersonal.

The second, related objection is that liberal egalitarianism is too morally focused on rights. Over the classical liberal support for rights to life, liberty, and property, liberal egalitarians endorse rights to "resources, capabilities, opportunities, and so on." While the greater scope of these rights claims is admirable, they are still rights claims, and this formulation, Marxists insist, precludes the necessary work of politicizing power relations. But Smith points out that liberal egalitarians were always aware that "rights are not constitutive properties possessed by individuals prior to entering into social and political relations." This means that, in fact, liberal egalitarians would usually be disposed to orient their arguments for rights in ways that would confront forms of domination. For instance, Ronald Dworkin was very critical of the *Citizens United* decision because it siphons excessive power to legal fictions like corporations in the name of "rights" to expression and speech. Smith also smartly points out that Marx's own view of rights is more complex than his usual critical disposition would suggest. Throughout his life Marx continued to argue for an expansion of liberal rights, particularly to suffrage, in no small part because he agreed with the liberal egalitarian conviction that winning certain kinds of rights do more than just secure individual autonomy. They can be politically and socially empowering.

Lastly, Smith points out that the standard Marxist objection that liberals crudely appeal to "nature" doesn't apply to liberal egalitarians. Once again, classical liberals like Locke and Hobbes would often appeal to fictional "states of nature" to justify their anthropological and political assumptions. One of the most pernicious and enduring impacts of which has been the reification of property as a natural institution, in the sense of being divorced from considerations of coercion and power. In fact, as many Marxists have pointed out, property entitlements often emerge as legal relations backed by state force imposed without deliberation by the population. But as Smith observes, "liberal egalitarians...explicitly acknowledge the historicity of both society and social theory." They acknowledge that material and power equality has never been the "natural" boon of humankind, and that property rights aren't natural human accessories but always political. All liberal egalitarians admire the history of political struggle for equality, and insist that inequalities that do persist in society need to serve some demonstrable good that outweighs the negative consequences.

Smith not only does a great job making clear to his fellow Marxists why liberal egalitarianism isn't just classical liberalism with a few modest innovations. He provides a very useful guide to liberal egalitarianism even for those within the tradition, surveying it with charity and economy.

The critique of liberal egalitarianism

After steel-manning liberal egalitarianism against its Marxist critics Smith goes on to ask whether it remains vulnerable to Marxist objections. He concludes that it does. Smith's main objection is that, for as many advances as liberal egalitarians have made, they still lack an adequate understanding of power relations created by capital and the state. One of the core Marxist insights is that human beings both create, and in turn are molded by, their social reality. Marx hoped that by exposing this recursive process through a "critique" of political economy, he would enable individuals — especially in the working classes — to become aware of it. But very often we instead become dominated by and alienated from the very social world we establish.

In capitalist societies, the emergent properties of capital eventually coalesce into something rather like an "Absolute Subject" that acts like an agent above and beyond the individual actions that make it up. This can be seen in how even powerful figures in the dominant classes retain their status and amplify economic power only through subordination to the imperatives of the market. This necessity of obeying market imperatives is, in Marx's view, a form of "tyranny" and it is made worse by the way we naturalize it and the forms of domination associated with it.

For instance, Marx highlights how the transition from feudal peasant labor to capitalist wage labor catalyzed and reflected a change in our ideological thinking. The loyal and dutiful peasant was replaced by the thrifty and hardworking laborer. Over time these comparatively small scale historical transitions led to world-changing qualitative transitions as feudal society gave way to the world of Bill Gates, Elon Musk, and Kylie Jenner. Still defined by inequality, capitalists remain compelled by the same kinds of social imperatives as their feudal ancestors. Worse still, the world of capitalism appears as immutable as its predecessors. Capital stands over the social world so long as the social forms of dissociated sociality remain in place, that is, so long as the individual in capitalism is "naked"; cut off from access to the material preconditions of human life, dependent on capital's permission to gain access to these preconditions. If, however, that particular form of social organization were to dissipate, capital, despite all its supposed powers, would dissipate immediately.

This leads individuals to develop a highly abstract, and even theological, way of reasoning and discussing their own social reality — discussing market "laws" and "imperatives" as though they operate on and through human beings rather than as a result of their willed decisions.

But far from a benign social tendency, Smith points out how this narrows the parameters of human understanding and blinds us to how the forms of exploitation and inequality engendered by capitalism inhibit human flourishing. This most severely impacts those who are most dominated by capitalism, those relegated to permanent disadvantage and precarity. But it also applies to privileged classes, who are subject to the same "tyranny of necessity" as poorer classes. It is not ultimately the ruling class of capitalists that is the target of Marxist animosity, since capitalists are as subject to the coercive imperatives of the market as anyone. For instance the comparatively low wages paid to workers isn't a consequence of capitalist greed, since many bosses may well be inclined to be generous. Instead it is a consequence of the market for labor, which can drive prices for work down even when individual capitalists may wish to offer a higher or living wage.

Smith allows that liberal egalitarians often are sensitive to the ways capital inhibits human flourishing, but lacking a sufficient understanding of it, their approaches to mitigating the damage are inadequate. Liberal egalitarian approaches often take the form of demanding redistribution by the state while holding that "capitalist market societies can further human agency and [flourish] when the proper background conditions are in place." These background conditions include providing extensive rights to a relative equality of resources or capabilities for all, not to mention rights to basic social services. Smith acknowledges that this would naturally be an improvement on our neoliberal status quo, but he argues it is insufficient, since by keeping the power of capital intact, the basic forces of coercion, global injustice, and economic instability will persist.

Consequently, Smith thinks we should still want to move "beyond liberal egalitarianism."

This echoes Marx's own critique of liberal socialists like John Stuart Mill. On Marx's interpretation, Mill thought that the manner in which production is carried out under capitalism isn't up for debate; it is subject to the laws of economics. We can only pose questions of distribution and redistribution. As he put it in the *Contribution to the Critique of Political Economy* "[for Mill]...production, as distinct from distribution, etc., is to be presented as governed by eternal natural laws which are independent of history, and at the same time bourgeois relations are clandestinely passed off as irrefutable natural laws of society *in abstracto*." But Marx felt that by retaining relations of production as they were, any effort to redistribute wealth would retain all the domination that came with capitalism. Mill's efforts — and liberal egalitarian efforts more broadly — to redistribute resources without addressing disparities in power that came from private ownership of the means of production would inevitably fail.

We can concede the partial truth of Marx's objection while stressing that it doesn't seem to have been empirically borne out. Welfarist efforts to humanize capitalism left many disparities of power intact, leaving the door open for the neoliberal turn of the 1970s and '80s and then the reactionary backlash of the 2010s. But a lot was also achieved in terms of securing higher standards of living, regulating dangers in the workplace, and even (for a time) setting up genuinely powerful labor movements. It strikes me that a sufficient quantity of major reforms could lead over time to a qualitative transformation. And this is where the argument for liberal egalitarianism comes in.

Conclusion: A liberal egalitarian response of Marxism

In fact, the realm of freedom actually begins only where labour which is determined by necessity and mundane considerations ceases; thus in the very nature of things it lies beyond the sphere of actual material production. Just as the savage must wrestle with Nature to satisfy his wants, to maintain and reproduce life, so must civilised man, and he must do so in all social formations and under all possible modes of production. With his development this realm of physical necessity expands as a result of his wants; but, at the same time, the forces of production which satisfy these wants also increase. Freedom in this field can only consist in socialised man, the associated producers, rationally regulating their interchange with Nature, bringing it under their common control, instead of being ruled by it as by the blind forces of Nature; and achieving this with the least expenditure of energy and under conditions most favourable to, and worthy of, their human nature. But it nonetheless still remains a realm of necessity. Beyond it begins that development of human energy which is an end in itself, the true realm of freedom, which, however, can blossom forth only with this realm of necessity as its basis. The shortening of the working-day is its basic prerequisite.

Karl Marx, Capital Vol III

Smith is absolutely right to criticize liberal egalitarians for having too narrow an understanding of capital, the state, and power generally. This cuts the other way too; Irving Howe rightly chastised socialists for being blasé about the kinds of state power liberals had very effectively analyzed and criticized for generations. But it'd be hard to deny that critical theorists from Marx onward have developed far more interesting and sophisticated accounts of history, power, and capital than many liberals.

Liberals have always had a leg up on Marxists in normative social theorizing, and it is here that a partial response to Smith's challenge can be formulated. I've used the republican term "domination" at several points in this essay to preface how it can be useful in helping liberals think through these issues. The republican tradition of non-domination was a deep influence on liberals and Marxists, and anticipates the core commitment to freedom and human flourishing common to both traditions at their best. Non-domination refers to the importance of being free from the arbitrary will of another. In contexts where, even if I'm routinely left to my own devices and earn enough to keep a roof over my head, most of the decisions in my life are set by an "Absolute subject" like capital and its laws, it is hard to say I am meaningfully free.

This can take on very tangible forms that are transparently noxious. Consider some of the examples given in Elizabeth Anderson's *Private Government*. When employees enter a twenty-first-century workplace, they're essentially subject to private dictatorships. Companies can decide when they go to the bathroom, what kinds of clothes they wear, what kinds of material they post on social media, the language they use, whether they choose to reproduce or not, where they commit their labor and how, and of course how profits are distributed. For far too long liberals have assumed that, since all this takes place in the "private" sphere and is voluntarily contracted into by employees and employers, the forms of domination aren't of serious concern. But as Anderson points out, if domination by state government is wrong because it constrains the freedom of individuals, liberals should at least be sensitive to the vulgarities inflicted by democratically unaccountable private government, especially since many of us spend most of our adult waking lives at work.

Take Rawls' point about how economic inequality tends to lead to political inequality. In his last book, *Justice as Fairness: A Restatement,* Rawls expressed an interest in moving toward "property owning democracy" or "liberal socialism." This was in part because he thought welfare statism didn't do enough to care for the least well-off to count as a just society. But it was also because he recognized how inequalities in economic power lead to people getting unequal value from their basic political liberties. This undermined the view that all of us are equal citizens of a democratic society, especially when legal fictions like corporations are effectively granted rights to spend on electioneering at the behest of their billionaire owners. Far from leading to workplace plutocracy, what we're faced with here is old-fashioned aristocracy rearing its head by another name — something liberals historically prided themselves on rebelling against.

My point in bringing up these examples isn't to provide a full response to Smith. It is instead to mobilize the resources of liberal egalitarianism to answer his challenge by modifying them with certain republican arguments that should be palatable to liberals and Marxists alike. And to do so in a way that doesn't require abandoning a commitment to many of the basic liberal rights which I think are so integral to any good society; which, to be clear, should include an unqualified right to personal property. But beyond that, I think liberal egalitarians and Marxists would agree that there is no need to make a fetish of expansive property or capital where that precludes interrogating the very real ways economic power leads to domination. We don't need to go beyond liberal egalitarianism. What we need to do is extend the principles of liberal egalitarianism to places where liberals have historically fallen silent.

CONCLUSION: DON'T RETVRN[1]

Reject modernity. Embrace tradition. So goes a beloved motto of the online right. At their crudest, these calls to abandon modernity seem a lot like mere nostalgia — a kind of barely thought-through instinct that the past was inherently better than a debased present. The easy thing to do, therefore, is to just go back to the past. Like a lot of easy answers to complex problems, "RETVRN"[2] is easy because it's lazy and wrong.

Thoughtful conservatives recognize this. In his 2009 essay "Progress and Memory," the Notre Dame political theorist and *Compact* contributing editor Patrick Deneen diagnosed "nostalgism" as a form of "temporal fragmentation that constitutes one of the features of the landscape of modernity." Deneen claimed the nostalgist makes the same mistake as the "progressive" in being "hostile to the lessons of history" through a kind of "willful forgetting." The nostalgist sees historical developments as nothing more than a litany of "human failure and misery" and ignores the

---

1   Reprinted from *Compact Magazine*.

2   RETVRN is a now common reactionary term referring to going back to a more idyllic past when men stayed men and women stayed down.

genuinely progressive advances modernity has achieved over premodernity.

While Deneen was surely correct in diagnosing "RETVRN" politics long before they took on that label, there is a more thoughtful rejection of modernity, long popular on the right, which can't be reduced to instinctual nostalgism and the paradoxical projection of utopian hopes onto a past that is to be restored as our future.

At their best, right-wing critics of the modern have offered deep arguments that the ethical or aesthetic core of modernity has robbed us of something we possessed in the past. Or even that modernity, for all its progressive aspirations, has a thinly concealed dark side that belies its claim to be an ethical or aesthetic advancement on premodernity. As the Canadian philosopher Charles Taylor powerfully argues, including in his most recent book, *Cosmic Connections*, these deeper critics are ultimately misguided, but their claims deserve far more serious consideration than those of your typical "RETVRN" trolls.

Two emblematic figures in this right-wing tradition are Fyodor Dostoevsky and Friedrich Nietzsche. These authors represent the very summit of right-wing thought, and it's hard to deny the potency of their critiques of the modern.

In classics like *Notes from Underground* and *The Brothers Karamazov*, Dostoevsky lamented how the modern world has made us materially better off and spiritually nihilistic. In *Notes*, published in 1864, he imagined the titular underground man vacillating between indulging his libertine desires without constraint and conceiving cosmic and social reality as a vast, deterministic prison from which there is no escape.

This was brought about by the spread of anti-religious scientific metaphysics. The new science — or perhaps it's better to say scientism — held that everything is scientifically predetermined. Yet this scientism was aligned in a tense combination with modernist political ideologies like liberalism and socialism that insisted the highest human aspiration was to do as one liked. But, asked the likes of Dostoevsky, how could this be? The elective affinity lay in this. If we all are just meaningless matter in motion, and everything is predetermined by the firing of minuscule particles, it follows that there is no soul to mutilate and no evil in being wretched to others. After all, science had also shown our basic nature to be irredeemably selfish and hedonistic. All that was left was to accept it as a fact of life.

In the final novels of his maturity, Dostoevsky refined this condemnation further. In *The Brothers Karamazov* (1880), the critique of modernity plays out in the tension between brothers Ivan and Alyosha. Alyosha is the less intellectually gifted of the two: kind, religious, invariably rural, and sentimentally attached to his family for all its flaws. Naturally, he wants to become a local Orthodox priest. By contrast, Ivan is a refined modernist intellectual who has thoroughly absorbed many of the new ideas about liberalism, socialism, science, and atheism streaming in from the West. And he is desperately unhappy for it; Ivan's thinking has reached such a refined point that any conviction he lays out for himself invariably twists back into its opposite.

Ivan's soul has become not a mystery but a poison to himself. He flirts with the nihilistic idea that "everything is permitted" in a godless world, but then makes clear that his rejection of God is less based on pure reason than the resentment of a divine being who would allow his children to suffer so much. These tensions never become resolved for Ivan, and that is the point: they can't be resolved. Like Kant's antinomies of reason, the ideas of modernity contradict and turn inward on themselves. In the end, Dostoevsky recommended the purer, innocent faith of

Alyosha as a surer route to happiness and human kindness than the grandly pitiful intellectualism of Ivan.

On the other front is Nietzsche, the German apostle of the death of God and a world beyond good and evil. Nietzsche deeply admired Dostoevsky, calling him the "only psychologist...from which I have anything to learn" in 1889's *Twilight of the Idols*. Nietzsche insisted relentlessly that modernity is radically nihilistic and becoming ever more so, as our species sleepwalks toward the era of the "last men," who will no great projects but are deeply concerned with "health."

What makes Nietzsche's thinking so frightening, even for many on the right, is its insistence that at the metaphysical and moral root of modernity's decline was Christianity. This renders his critique radically different from that of many other conservatives and reactionaries, for whom a hierarchical and orderly Christianity was and remains the antidote to decadent liberalism and socialism. By contrast, Nietzsche insisted that it was Christianity's moral insistence on spiritual equality and respect for the weak and poor that laid the seeds for the emergence of doctrines like liberalism, socialism, and democracy.

Radical progressives like Frantz Fanon agreed with Christ that the "wretched of the earth" must know that God is on their side, that history will vindicate their ascendency. In this respect, modernity and modern political ideologies didn't represent a rupture with Christianity but a sometimes banal, sometimes fanatical effort to carry on the Christian moral project in secular terms. The woke may not believe in Jesus, but many of them unwittingly carry out his message — a lot like how some Fox News pundits insist we should believe in Christ while closing their ears to the message of the Good Samaritan. For Nietzsche, this posture was unacceptable, since it meant a continuation of the spiral into nihilism cultivated by Christian morality and its offshoots: reverence for the weak and unhealthy, rule by the slaves, and the promulgation mediocre values that could never become life-affirming.

Nietzsche's own solution to the problem of modernity was to call for an aristocratic rejuvenation. Albeit not one that would merely restore a kind of flat Homeric ideal, let alone a conservative rejuvenation of the *ancien régimes* of Europe. Instead, Nietzsche wanted what Georg Brandes called a form of "aristocratic radicalism" that would be both new, awe-inspiring, and terrifying. Not coincidentally, Nietzsche insisted in his final text, *Ecce Homo*, published posthumously in 1908, that great politics would begin with him. The wars and genocides of the first half of the twentieth century gave humanity a horrifying glimpse of what such "great politics" might look like (notwithstanding Nietzsche's efforts to distance himself from the nascent Teutonic and anti-Semitic passions of the nineteenth century).

Nietzsche's great insight, shared by all the right's sharpest commentators, is that it is impossible to quarantine premodernity from modernity, to insist that the latter is some radical break or fall. For instance, if it is true that Christianity is a religion of world-historic influence, then the current shift against Christian morality didn't emerge from without. Rather, the historical potential to reject Christianity came at least in part from within the Christian tradition itself.

In *The Genealogy of Morals* (1887), Nietzsche pointed out how a Platonic will to truth eventually led Christian thinkers to ask the fatal question about the truth of their own doctrine. Similarly, the ethical traditions so despised by the right — liberalism, socialism, feminism, and the like — aren't a break from Western civilization. They emerged as expressions of its internal cultural dynamics, and have roots dating back millennia to the egalitarianism of Christianity and Stoicism, the idealism of Platonism, and so on.

For those who can't reconcile themselves to modernity, this poses serious and anxious puzzles. But a better path forward is to stop trying to reject modernity as some kind of aberration and instead recognize it as a valuable and shared part of our heritage. Indeed, we might even go further and describe how the ethics and aesthetics of modernity constitute an advance on what came before — one that, of course, owes a debt to the past, but an advance, all the same.

This is the longstanding argument of the Canadian philosopher Charles Taylor, including in his new book, *Cosmic Connections: Poetry in the Age of Disenchantment*. Taylor argues that premodernity is often nostalgized as a time of greater cosmic and social order. Every single thing was put into its place by nature or God and had a teleological role to fulfill. In some respects, the feelings of "disenchantment" many of us feel about modernity emerges from this loss of integration into a cosmic and social whole, along with the attendant certainty about our ends.

Taylor is sympathetic to these feelings. *Cosmic Connections* is often a rumination on reactionary poets like Baudelaire and T.S. Eliot, who articulated these feelings of disenchantment and alienation beautifully. But what they failed to acknowledge, Taylor insists, is that premodernity's sense of order came at an enormous ethical price — one so high no ethical person could now pay it or wish to do so.

The social vision of the era was defined by what Taylor described as "hierarchical complementarity" in his 2003 book, *Modern Social Imaginaries*. Each person occupied a place on the social pyramid, which meant that no one was considered equal in terms of dignity or entitlement to concern. Some lives, indeed some groups of people, were simply more valuable than others, which entitled elites not only to rule but even to wield life-or-death power over their subjects. The end result wasn't, in fact, glorious and orderly societies but regimes under which hundreds of thousands would die so the Sun King could win the Duchy of Lorraine and enrich the House of Bourbon. Or worse, slave societies where some were considered natural inferiors ordained to serve their racial betters until the whip and exhaustion wore out their uses.

Against this backdrop, Taylor urges us to recognize how the ethics of modernity represent real "growth" over what came before. This doesn't mean that individual human beings are any better or worse than they've ever been; we were and will remain sinful creatures, as the Augustinian tradition teaches. But the "ideal forms" of our societies are more ethically demanding and impressive than what one found in premodernity. Indeed, one of the reasons for the widespread sense of alienation in today's societies is precisely that modern ethics demands we do so much more for all than premodern ethics, which leads many to rightly feel that we are not living up to our own states' ideals. Taylor calls this the more "acute angle of transcendence" characteristic of modern society, which it is much steeper for us to climb.

Consider migration. Pre-modern social imaginaries do offer some support for showing generosity to the foreign "other." For instance, in Leviticus the Hebrews are commanded to not mistreat foreigners who live upon their lands, and to remember that they were once also refugees in the land of Egypt. Still, the thrust of the premodern tradition was that the newcomer had no serious claims upon the society that had admitted him beyond charity — and could also eject or deny him equal rights at will. By contrast, modern ethics has a universalistic quality in insisting it is equally important that every person's life — whether American, Mexican or Haitian — go well. This means we have duties to treat each person as possessing a dignity that places her beyond price, as Kant would put it, and we cannot allow morally arbitrary factors like national citizenship or ethnicity to determine what we owe her.

This is, of course, an extraordinarily demanding ideal. So demanding that many conservatives, like Pat Buchanan, characterize it as utopian and unrealistic. But that's just the point. This modern ethical ideal is harder to realize than the premodern one because it is *higher*. By contrast, for all the moralism that the most fanatical right-wingers indulge in, there is a real sense in which their premodern insistence on treating nationals better than others is much easier — because it asks far less of them. They want to buy their sense of moral certainty through chauvinistic nationalism and the prioritization of us over others; in other words, they want to buy it on the (very) cheap. In this respect, the funny spectacle of Trumpians insisting that Haitian migrants are eating cats and dogs is representative of a predictable ethical decline into the unseriousness of easy nationalism. Tribalism may be rooted in human nature, but it's the hard task of living up to the better angels of that nature that makes a country just.

Where, then, does this put us in relation to sharper reactionary critics of modernity like Dostoevsky and Nietzsche? Such figures were right to diagnose modernity as a time of alienation, but wrong to assume the problem lies in modern ethics. The answer to these feelings of alienation isn't to abandon a demanding ethics for one that is easier á la Dostoevsky's romantic Christian traditionalism, or to seek to fulfill the Nietzschean ideal of the radical aristocrat (which is bound to lead to monstrous politics of power and eugenic domination). The answer, rather, is to undertake the immensely difficult task of making the modern world live up to its commitments; to really achieve a society in which each person has an equal chance to lead a good life. That we are so far from this is a reminder of the incompleteness of the modern project. We have much still to achieve.

REPEATER BOOKS

is dedicated to the creation of a new reality. The landscape of twenty-first-century arts and letters is faded and inert, riven by fashionable cynicism, egotistical self-reference and a nostalgia for the recent past. Repeater intends to add its voice to those movements that wish to enter history and assert control over its currents, gathering together scattered and isolated voices with those who have already called for an escape from Capitalist Realism. Our desire is to publish in every sphere and genre, combining vigorous dissent and a pragmatic willingness to succeed where messianic abstraction and quiescent co-option have stalled: abstention is not an option: we are alive and we don't agree.